THE THEATRE ROYAL

BRIGHTON

Books by Antony Dale

Fashionable Brighton, 1820–1860
The History and Architecture of Brighton
About Brighton
Brighton Old and New
Brighton Town and Brighton People
James Wyatt, Architect

THE THEATRE ROYAL BRIGHTON

by

ANTONY DALE

ORIEL PRESS
STOCKSFIELD
HENLEY BOSTON LONDON

First published in 1980
by Oriel Press Ltd. (Routledge & Kegan Paul Ltd.)
Branch End, Stocksfield,
Northumberland, NE43 7NA

Printed in Great Britain
by Knight & Forster Ltd., Leeds

ISBN 0 85362 185 3

CONTENTS

ILLUSTRATIONS

DEDICATION

In memory of my old friend
Geoffrey Carrington, who loved the
Theatre Royal and would have been
very interested in this book,

and

for his and my good friends,
Harold and Irene Farncombe.

ACKNOWLEDGEMENTS

IN WRITING this book my principal debt is to the Management of the Theatre Royal and in particular to the Managing Director, Mr Melville Gillam, for giving me access to the archives of the theatre. These consist mainly of the minutes of the Directors' and shareholders' meetings of Brighton Theatre Royal Limited since its inception in 1889 and the programmes of the plays staged at the theatre. But the latter do not go back farther than 1935. Two other Directors of the theatre have been most helpful: Lady Cohen of Brighton with advice in the early stages and Mr R. C. Pascoe for allowing me to inspect the deeds of the theatre and the adjoining buildings owned by the theatre that are in the custody of his firm, Howlett and Clarke. Mr L. H. Elliott of Russell, Ohly and Company, who is Secretary of both Brighton Theatre Royal Limited and the Theatre Royal Brighton (Stage Plays) Limited, kindly gave me information about the inter-relation of these two companies.

Several past Directors of Brighton Theatre Royal Limited have provided me with most useful information. The Director to whom I am most endebted is Mr Glynne Burnand who was a Director from 1948 to 1971 and has probably a more detailed knowledge of the theatre than anyone not now actually on the staff of management. Mr E. Infield Willis, who was Chairman of the same Company from 1942 to 1963 kindly gave me information about his grandfather, Henry John Infield, who was the first Chairman of the Company. Mr George Scatliff also was most helpful.

Past and present employees of the theatre have been able to give me very valuable information of a different kind. The late Jack Keates during the twenty-eight years of his connection with the theatre compiled a large collection of material relating to the theatre: Theatre Royaliana it might be called. His widow, Mrs Winifred Keates, has very kindly allowed me to look through this, with most valuable results, and to reproduce certain items from it. I am grateful to Miss Ann Travers, the present Manager of the theatre, for information about Baxter Somerville and to Mrs Enid Armstrong of the Box Office staff for similar details about Lawson Lambert.

To Mr Douglas King, who is in charge of the maintenance of the theatre, I am endebted for information about the geography of the dressing-rooms and the back-stage premises which has saved me from making several mistakes.

A quite remarkable source of information about the running of the theatre in the last seventy years has come from Mr George Pennifold, now aged 89, the oldest surviving member of the theatre's staff, who remembers not only Lawson Lambert but even H. Cecil Beryll. He has related to me several old-world details of considerable interest. I was also able to have several conversations before her death with the late Mrs Violet Helliwell who was for so long a programme seller in the theatre. I only regret that I had no opportunity to do likewise with the late Mr Bill Tupper, the commissionaire.

I was fortunate enough to establish contact with descendants of Henry John and Ellen Elizabeth Nye Chart. Their granddaughter, Mrs Cynthia Williams, was indefatigable in answering questions about her family. I am also endebted to the Nye Chart's great-grandson, Mr D. P. Kindersley, and his wife for the loan of material relating to the Nye Charts.

Finally I must record my thanks to Dame Flora Robson for talking to me about her visits to the Theatre Royal.

INTRODUCTION

THE THEATRE ROYAL at Brighton is one of the most distinguished provincial theatres in Great Britain. It is an elegant building which has been listed by the Secretary of State for the Department of the Environment as a building of special architectural or historic interest. The auditorium is excellent for both sight and sound. In spite of the pillars remaining from the rebuilding of 1866 it is possible to see and hear well from every seat in the theatre. But much more important than this is the fact that it has that indefinable quality *atmosphere*. This is discernible to both playgoers and actors, as many a speech by leading actors from the stage has emphasized. Much of this magic comes from the knowlege that every leading British actor and actress from Sarah Siddons until today has appeared on its stage, with the single exception of Sir Squire Bancroft who seems never to have played there. Several distinguished actors, singers and dancers from other countries have also graced its boards. It has been throughout its life a theatre to which eminent players have liked to return, despite the alleged reserve of Brighton first-night audiences. It is possible, that more prior-to-London productions have been tried out there than in any other theatre in England.

All this has immensely enriched the quality of life in Brighton. Second only to the Royal Pavilion, the Theatre Royal is the greatest amenity which Brighton holds for both inhabitants and visitors alike. It has had its ups and downs, as the story related in this book shows. On several occasions the people of Brighton who valued the theatre have trembled at the possibility of its closing, when theatres in other towns were suffering a similar fate. At the present time its future seems reasonably secure. Long may it remain so to delight the audiences of other periods than our own, as it has enthralled me since the first performance I attended in

1922, of which I still have the programme!

In writing this book I have tried to interweave three separate strands of the theatre's history which all seem to me of some interest. The first is the building itself. This has gone through several phases of development and is not all of one piece. The second comprises the people who have owned and managed the theatre. Many of these were characters of considerable interest in their own right. Two of them — Mrs Nye Chart and Baxter Somerville — were quite remarkable. They and the policy which they pursued for the theatre have given it a reputation of far greater than local status, so that even outside Brighton it is still today accounted one of the most notable theatres in the country. Third and most important of all, there are the actors and actresses who have played in the theatre and the plays in which they have appeared. Naturally it has not been possible to mention every one of those who have made a theatrical name at any period or to record every single appearance of even the greatest players. Any such account would degenerate into a boring catalogue. But my aim has been to bring out enough individual names to show that this theatre has been a microcosm of stage life from 1807 until today and that in every period whoever were the stars of the day have appeared on the Brighton stage. I have also tried to note when such actors or dramatists had other special connections with Brighton, and it is quite surprising how many of them have done so. The existence of the theatre itself has set up almost a virtuous circle in attracting the theatrical world to Brighton and Brighton to the theatre.

CHAPTER I

EARLY BRIGHTON THEATRES, 1764—1807

BY THE end of the eighteenth century most towns of any size had a theatre where performances were held from time to time when companies of strolling players arrived on a visit. Prior to Dr Russell's discovery of Brightholmston the town was too small to have such a building. But as the fashionable world began to frequent his new spa the need for a theatre arose. The first person to cater for this need was Charles Johnson, who was already the proprietor of theatres at Salisbury, Chichester and Portsmouth.[1] He adapted for the purpose a barn in Brightholmston which stood on the west side of Old Steine, near to the Castle Hotel. The first performance there was given on 7th November 1764. Thereafter Johnson's company returned to Brightholmston each year and in 1770 performed three days a week at 1 p.m. and, on wet days when carriage exercise was impossible, at 12 noon. The season was very short as the tenancy of the building ended when it was required for the purpose of bringing in the harvest. The last performance there was of *The Merry Wives of Windsor* on 30th August 1770. When the theatre closed it was announced that the company was moving to another barn elsewhere on the Steine. No record exists as to whether this move ever took place or where the other barn stood.

No more theatrical performances were held in Brighton for four years. The next enterprise was a more permanent venture. In 1774 a bricklayer named Samuel Paine built a theatre in North Street for Roger Johnstone, who had formerly been the property man at Covent Garden Theatre. The first performance there was of *The Jealous Wife* by George Colman on 30th August of that year. In 1777 Johnstone leased the theatre to Joseph Fox, a tavern-keeper

[1] The Chichester theatre was opened in 1764. It was rebuilt in 1791, but the building of that date still exists as number 43 South Street.

of Covent Garden, for fifteen years at the rent of £60 a year. In this theatre Sophia Baddeley, Mary (or Perdita) Robinson, John Quick, Dudley West Digges and — by tradition — David Garrick appeared. It was first patronised by royalty in the person of the Duke of Cumberland, brother of George III, in 1779. The Prince of Wales attended frequently after his first visit to Brighton in 1783. In 1786 the building was refitted internally. But a quarrel arose between the Manager, Joseph Fox, and the proprietor, Samuel Paine. As a result Fox made application to the Lewes Magistrates to transfer his licence to another building at the north-west end of Duke Street in Brighton. This was not opposed by Paine. As a result the licence of the North Street building lapsed. It was closed in 1789 and subsequently converted into the printing office of William and Arthur Lee, later Wallis's wine vaults.

With the Duke Street theatre we enter the realm of visual records as a print of this by T. Woodfall of Villiers Street, The Strand, exists, which was reproduced in Bishop's *Brighton in the Olden Time*. The building had a blind façade fronted with weather-boarding, grooved or rusticated in imitation of masonry. Its only architectural feature was a wide porch of Tuscan columns with a pediment above. This porch gave direct entrance to the boxes. The designer was named Still and the builder Stephen Poune. The cost was approximately £2,500. According to Erredge's *History of Brighton* a private Act of Parliament was passed in 1788 to authorise the opening of this theatre.

The first performance was of *The West Indian* by Richard Cumberland and *Barnaby Brittle*, adapted from Thomas Betterton's *Amorous Widow*, which were given on 13th July 1790. Amongst the performers who appeared at this theatre were: John and Charles Kemble; their sister Sarah Siddons; Dorothy Jordan; Harriot Mellon, who later married in succession the banker, Thomas Coutts, and the ninth Duke of St. Albans; the Chevalier d' Éon, who gave fencing displays in women's clothing; and the singers John Brahan, Nancy Starace, Michael Kelly and Anna Maria Crouch. Michael Kelly was a well-known baritone who, before becoming the resident composer at Drury Lane theatre, had had a distinguished career at the Imperial Opera House in

Plate 1.
Print of theatre in Duke Street.
(Reproduced by kind permission of the Director of the Brighton Art Gallery.)

Vienna. There he had appeared in the original production of *The Marriage of Figaro*, in which he doubled the parts of Don Basilio and the notary, Don Curzio, in the last act. In the latter part as a piece of stage 'business' he gave the character a stammer, against the opposition of Mozart himself at first. But it proved so successful that the stammer has almost invariably been adopted by the singers who have played the part since then, as if it were part of the stage directions. Kelly had frequently sung with Nancy Starace in many opera houses in Europe. With Anna Maria Crouch in Brighton he played Macheath and she Polly Peachum in *The Beggars' Opera*. He and Mrs Crouch were for many years lovers and had a house in Brighton first at No. 9 Mulberry Square, North Street, and later on the West Cliff. Mrs Crouch died on 2nd October 1805 and was buried in St Nicholas's church-yard, Brighton where Kelly erected a Coadeware stone urn to her memory, backing onto the wall of Church Street.

Joseph Fox died in 1792, and his widow sold the theatre a few years later to Hewitt Cobb of Sydenham. A whole series of different managements ensued until, in 1804, there appeared the next person who was important in the theatre's history, John Brunton Senior. He was the son of a soapmaker at Norwich who started life as a grocer and tea dealer in Drury Lane, London. He subsequently became an actor and appeared at Covent Garden Theatre. Then he went back to Norwich and became a member of the stock company there. He also played at Bath. Eventually he became the Manager of the Norwich acting circuit. No explanation is available of his transfer to Brighton. But under his management the Duke Street theatre made headway. On 12th July 1805 the Prince of Wales made some kind of official visit, though not his first visit, to the theatre, and thereafter the name of the Theatre Royal was adopted. A special box was created for him which was decorated with sparkling gold stars and festoons of roses on panels of a dark blue ground and furnished with handsome painted chairs, a rich carpet and a crimson velvet curtain. However, despite this success Hewitt Cobb and John Brunton had decided to move elsewhere. The season of 1806 was the last in Duke Street, and on 21st April 1807 the premises were sold for demolition, with the fittings auctioned separately in lots.

CHAPTER II

THE FIRST THEATRE IN NEW ROAD, 1807–1854

In 1800 the north end of Great East Street, as East Street was then called, ran almost directly under the western windows of the Royal Pavilion — Holland's classical Pavilion. It is true that the Prince of Wales had, since 1795, rented a piece of land to the west of this road which was then known as the dairy field. This had been part of the farmland of the 'respectable farmhouse' — Grove House — which the Prince had at first rented and which became the nucleus of the Royal Pavilion. But this land was not of much use to him as long as it was separated from his house by the line of a public road. On 25th August 1803 he therefore came to an agreement with the Town Commissioners whereby he was given permission to close the northern end of Great East Street in exchange for the provision of other land to the west on which to make a new road. With this purpose in mind the Prince purchased the dairy field in December 1803 for £4,200; the land immediately adjoining it on the west, which was then occupied as a public garden known as the Promenade Grove, in August 1802 for £3,500, plus £1,000 for the entrance to this from North Street; a narrow strip further west known as the Quakers' Croft or burial-ground in February 1806 for £800; and to the west again a garden belonging to John and Thomas Furner in January 1804 for £3,000.

It was through the centre of Furner's garden that the new road was constructed in 1806 under the supervision of William Porden, who was then building for the Prince the Stables and Riding House of the Pavilion (now the Dome and Corn Exchange). Some of the work was done by soldiers. The road was called New Road. Bond Street further west already existed but had been renamed New Street in 1794. It subsequently reverted to its original name to avoid confusion between the two parallel streets.

To recoup himself for these extensive purchases of land the Prince sold off some plots on each side of the new road. Two of these with a frontage of a hundred feet in the centre of the west side he conveyed on lease for 999 years for the sum of £1,250 to Hewitt Cobb, the proprietor of the theatre in Duke Street. The agreement to sell the land was dated 9th September 1806. £500 was paid on the signing of this contract, and receipt of this was acknowledged by William Porden's Clerk, Richard Hunt. One plot comprised the land on which the theatre was built, and the other the land immediately to the north of it. A few years later Cobb re-let this second plot for 99 years to John Field who, in 1821, built three houses on it, now Nos 13, 14 and 15 New Road.

The plans of the proposed theatre were to be approved by the Prince of Wales before it was built. This approval must have been given at once as the building was completed and opened by 6th June following. The conveyances were not in fact engrossed until after the opening of the theatre. They were dated 23rd and 24th July 1807 respectively and bear the Prince's signature. This was witnessed by Charles Bicknell and Colonel George Leigh, one of the Prince's Equerries, who that very year married Byron's half sister, Augusta.

The theatre was immediately let for £850 a year for two years to the former lessee of the old theatre in Duke Street, John Brunton Senior, whose address was then given as Cleveland Court, St. James's Street, London, and his son of the same name of Russell Street, Covent Garden. But Hewitt Cobb seems to have overtaxed his resources in building the theatre for, no sooner was it completed and open, than he disposed of a share in it. On 13th August 1807 he sold by auction at the Castle Hotel, Brighton, a half-share in the theatre, its contents, properties and costumes. This was bought for £5,512 10s. 0d. by Sir Thomas Clarges, Baronet, of Sutton-upon-Derwent, Yorkshire, and was conveyed to him on 30th August. He subsequently mortgaged this half-share for £1,500 but repaid £1,400 of this during his life. The remaining £100 was paid off after his death by the executors of his estate.

Several drawings and one very early photograph of this original theatre in New Road exist. The show it as an elegant classical building with a stuccoed front of three storeys. It was of three bays

Plate 2.
The Theatre of 1807, Photograph taken before 1866.
(Reproduced by kind permission of Mr. Philippe Garner.)

in width, the centre bay being wider than the others, and each flanked by pilasters which formed two narrow strips with a wider recessed portion in the centre. Over the whole was a parapet with panels of balustrading. The first floor windows had solid wooden shutters and recessed semi-circular tympana. The second floor windows were inserted within circular recesses. The main feature of the building was the Doric colonnade across the whole length of the ground floor. This contained five bays, the centre one flanked by single square columns, the two outer ones on each side by pairs of similar columns. Pendant lamps hung in the centre and end bays. Above the columns in the entablature were decorative recessed rectangles and in the centre the single word 'Theatre'. At this stage the building was in fact generally known as 'the new theatre' without capitals. But by the time that the Brighton artist W. A. Delamotte painted the building in 1855 the word 'Royal' had been added to the inscription in the entablature. There were five doorways behind the colonnade of which the centre one led into the boxes, those on the right into the pit and those on the left into the gallery. To the right of the building was an alleyway or twitten which led to the Manager's house behind.

The colonnade of the Theatre Royal subsequently set an example for most of the west side of New Road. In September 1820 Messrs Gotobed and Newnham were granted permission by the Town Commissioners to continue the colonnade westwards to North Street and round the corner as far as New Street, as Bond Street was then called, provided that this was twelve feet high and not wider than the pavement. The new construction in time came to be called the Royal Colonnade. It comprised Ionic columns with a series of wide bulging bow windows on the first floor above. It only survives in its original condition in front of Nos 6 and 7 New Road. Across the frontage of the theatre itself the colonnade was replaced in a more imposing but less elegant Corinthian version flush with the colonnade of the rest of the street, when the theatre was enlarged in 1894. The remainder of the colonnade in New Road and North Street was demolished at various dates down to about 1929.

There is no record of the architect of this first theatre. The design could possibly have been due to the same hand as produced the Theatre Royal at Worthing, which was opened in the same year and was not dissimilar in style. The architects of this were said to be 'Messrs Hides'. One naturally thinks also of Amon Wilds who, either alone or with his partner, Charles Augustus Busby, or his son, Amon Henry Wilds, was responsible for so many of the best Regency buildings in Brighton. But Wilds seems not to have come to Brighton from Lewes until 1814.

There is no pictorial representation of what the interior looked like. But we know that it was horseshoe-shaped and had two tiers of boxes, or galleries as they would now be called, of which the face was richly moulded. The Prince of Wales's box was on the left of the stage and was divided from the other boxes by a gilded grille, such as can still be seen in the royal box at Versailles and in other surviving eighteenth century court theatres. The ceiling was divided into nine panels representing Comedy, Tragedy, Terpsichore, Music, Love, Poetry, Geography and History, surrounded with gold ornamental scrolls interlaced with flowers. The theatre is said, surprisingly, to have accommodated 1,200 people. The house was illuminated by a range of patent lamps at the foot of the stage and by nine cut-glass chandeliers containing candles.

Almost all the architectural features of this first theatre in New Road were obliterated in the later rebuilding. In fact, probably the only survival is the staircase at the back of the stalls which leads to the dress circle. This is now a subsidiary staircase but was then the principal means of approaching the upper level. It has two niches on it, one of which contains a statue of Bacchus. This gives more the impression of a Regency than a Victorian production.

The first performance took place on 6th June 1807. The play was *Hamlet* with Charles Kemble in the title role and Maria Theresa de Camp, who was to marry Charles Kemble the following month, as Ophelia. John Brunton junior played Laertes. On 6th August a benefit performance was given under the patronage of Mrs Fitzherbert in aid of the widow and children of Nat Harman, a fisherman who had recently been drowned at sea. The proceeds of this amounted to £93.

Mrs Siddons made her first appearance in the theatre in August 1809. She played a number of parts: Lady Macbeth, Elvira in Sheridan's *Pizarro*, Mrs Beverley in *The Gamester* by James Shirley, Margaret of Anjou in *The Earl of Warwick* by the Rev. W. Franklin, Isabella in *The Fatal Marriage* by Thomas Southerne, Alicia in *Jane Shore* by Nicholas Rowe, Lady Randolph in *Douglas* by the Rev. John Hume and the Countess in *The Stranger* by Benjamin Thompson. Michael Kelly, John Brahan and Madame Catâlani all sang and Joseph Grimaldi, Charles Mathews and Dorothy Jordan all acted in the theatre in these years from 1807 to 1813.

When Sir Thomas Clarges bought a half-share in the theatre he entered into an agreement with Hewitt Cobb that, when the Bruntons' lease ended on 31st October 1809, he and Cobb would consult together concerning the letting and management of the theatre. There is no evidence as to whether in fact they did so or not. John Brunton Senior survived as a lessee until 1811 but for the last two years seems to have been in partnership with John Field. Brunton died in 1822. Their successors were W. Powell and Holland and then Jonas and Penley. A man called Groves of even less merit followed in 1813. The *Brighton Herald* referred to these managements as 'needy tenants at will' and said that their behaviour produced 'scenes of individual misery and turpitude'. The paper was particularly referring to Groves who on 3rd October 1813 decamped in the night, leaving the company unpaid. This was the first of several occasions in the history of the theatre in which such an incident occurred.

Groves's hurried departure made way for the first person of real significance in the theatre's history: Thomas Trotter. He was born in Gravesend, Kent, in 1779 and became an actor — no doubt one of those strolling players whose life was so precarious in the eighteenth century and whom we have already seen at the Brighton theatre. The first record of his appearance on the stage dates from 1802. By then he had his own company which, in that year, played in a barn theatre at Worthing. In the next few years this Company visited theatres in Petworth, Horsham, Chichester, Arundel, Littlehampton, Sevenoaks, Malling, Maidstone, Gravesend, Rochester, Milton Regis near Sittingbourne, Faversham, Canterbury, Hythe and Southend. Amongst these places, Trotter had leases at one time or other of theatres in Arundel, Horsham and Malling.

He seems first to have played in Brighton 17th December 1807, when his Company gave a performance and paid all the expenses in aid of the widows and orphans of fishermen lost in a great storm in the Channel on 19th November. He made another appearance on 22nd August 1809 in *Pizarro*, when he played Rollo opposite Mrs Siddons's Elvira. But between these two dates he had greatly improved his status as he had himself built four theatres: at Hythe, Southend, Gravesend and Worthing. Together with his rented theatres these formed a circuit for his company. The Hythe and Southend theatres opened in 1804 and were managed by Thomas Trotter until 1813 and 1812 respectively The first of these he eventually sold for £480 in 1826.

But probably the most important of his ventures was the Theatre Royal (as it later came to be called) in Ann Street, Worthing. This was built in 1806–7 and opened on 7th July 1807 with a performance of *The Merchant of Venice*, having Mrs Siddons as Portia, and her son Henry as Shylock. Thomas Trotter himself played Bassanio.

The Theatre Royal at Worthing, designed by 'Messrs Hides', was an elegant little building with a portico of four Doric columns projecting across the pavement, a niche in the centre of the first floor containing a bust of Shakespeare and circular window over it. Immediately adjoining the theatre to the south-east Trotter built himself a charming little Regency cottage orné of one storey with a projecting canopy. This was called Omega Cottage. Here he lived until his death in 1851.

From the circumstances of Trotter's life, from all contemporary references to him and, indeed, from some of his own recorded remarks, it is clear that he was a man not only of substance who made business-like arrangements but also a man of integrity. This is shown by the fact that in April 1814, when he applied to Quarter Sessions at Lewes for a licence to re-open the theatre, his application was supported by Sir Thomas Clarges who owned a half-share in the theatre, by the Earl of Egremont who was Lord Lieutenant of Sussex, and by the Churchwardens, the Overseer of the poor-rate and the High Constable of Brighton. He obtained a lease for five years at a rent of £600 a year. The theatre was redecorated throughout. The columns supporting the galleries of boxes were treated to imitate Siena marble. The front of the boxes had white panelling with gold mouldings, and the field in the centre was coloured pink with embossed floral decoration in gold. The cornice between the two galleries had a white frieze with burnished gold stars. When the weather became cold patent stoves were inserted to heat the house. The prices were 5s. 0d. for the boxes, 2s. 6d. for the pit and 1s. 0d. for the gallery.

The season opened on 23rd July 1814. When the curtain rose Thomas Trotter advanced to the front of the stage, explained his intentions and gave an undertaking that all claims against the theatre would be settled punctually every Saturday if these were brought to his personal attention. This promise was duly honoured. The National Anthem was then played, almost as a Te Deum to welcome the arrival of an honest man in the theatre. The company went on to give two plays: *The Honey Moon* by John Tobin and *The Review* by George Colman the younger. The season lasted until December. It had begun in what Porter's *History of the Theatres of Brighton from 1774 to 1885* called 'wretchedly depressing circumstances' but proved very successful as the takings exceeded those of 1813 by £700. This was no doubt due to the fact that Trotter was able to show his productions in Brighton and Worthing alternatively. During the five years of his tenancy he was able to secure the patronage not only of the Prince Regent but also of the Dukes of York, Clarence and Cumberland, of Princess Augusta and of Mrs Fitzherbert.

To supplement Trotter's permanent company at the Brighton and Worthing theatres visits were made by distinguished actors and actresses from London. Edmund Kean made his first appearance on 11th October 1814 in *Richard III* and returned several times, playing many of his principal roles such as Othello, Macbeth, Shylock and Sir Giles Overreach in *A New Way to Pay Old Debts* by Philip Massenger. Mrs Siddons, Charles Kemble and Charles Mathews all came; also Eliza O'Neill who, from 1814 to 1819, had a sparkling career as a tragedienne before marrying William Wrixon Becher, an Irish land-owner and Member of Parliament who subsequently inherited a baronetcy.

Amongst the well-known names was the famous or possibly ridiculous amateur actor named Robert Coates, who was generally known as Romeo Coates from his original appearance in *Romeo and Juliet*. He was renowned for the extravagance of his costume and is said to have worn jewelry worth £5,000 when appearing on the stage. He made three appearances in Brighton, on 23rd, 24th and 25th November 1815. On the first occasion, when he played the part of Captain Belcour, he wore a magnificent crimson velvet coat with real gold buttons, a white satin vest, diamonds and a gold-hilted dress sword ornamented with diamonds. On the third night in the play *West Indian* someone threw two chestnuts on the stage. He was so disconcerted by this that he temporarily retired from the scene. He later came back and denounced the offender from the stage. The audience appeared to sympathise with him, and an uproar ensued. Coates then left the theatre, so the play could not be resumed. But a farce *Love, Life and Physic* concluded the evening's proceedings. Coates subsequently offered a reward of £500 for the discovery of the offender, whom he threatened to drag onto the stage in order to receive the reproaches of the public. But needless to say no-one was ever discovered. Coates lived until 1848 and died as the result of a carriage accident, aged 75.

Thomas Trotter's seasons in the Brighton theatre at first ran from July (or in one instance June) until December. But from 1816 onwards he extended the run to the January or February of the following year. Extra stoves were inserted to heat the house. In his speech from the stage on 4th February 1817, which was the last night of the season, he said that the extension had not been a success. But it seems to have been repeated in the next years.

The ensuing period of closure in 1817 was used to refurbish the theatre. As the season of 1817–1818 drew to an end a rumour circulated that Trotter was in financial difficulties and that the actors of his theatre had not been paid. At the last performance in January he publicly denied this from the stage.

Mrs Odell in her book *The Theatre Royal 1814—19. Mr Trotter of Worthing and the Brighton Theatre* says that gas was first used to light the Brighton theatre in 1818. Unfortunately this statement cannot be checked as no other authority makes any reference to the instalment of gas. But one must perhaps accept the claim with a certain reserve as, if true, then the Theatre Royal was most certainly the first theatre in England in which this form of illumination was inserted and also the first building in Brighton to be lit by gas. Drury Lane and Covent Garden Theatres did not have gas until 1820 nor the Haymarket Theatre until 1843. In Brighton one would expect the Royal Pavilion to be the first in this field, and gas was not installed there until 1821. The streets of Brighton were first gas-lit in 1825. But even if 1818 is too good to be true, it is evident that the Brighton theatre was a very early example of such lighting either in a theatre or in a provincial town. The principal chandelier, when erected, could be raised and lowered at will over the centre of the pit. But it was soon removed as it detracted from the scenic effect of the stage and its great heat incommoded the occupants of the gallery.

The last performance under Thomas Trotter's management, which was also his benefit, took place on 1st February 1819. In his speech from the stage he regretted that his efforts had not been successful. By this he must have meant that his success was not great enough to encourage him to renew his lease of the building after five years for, in comparison to the seasons that preceded and followed his tenancy, the results were highly satisfactory.

He continued to manage the Worthing theatre until 1825. The following year he attempted to sell all his four theatres. But the only sale which actually went through was that at Hythe. Those at Worthing, Gravesend and Southend were still in his ownership at the time of his death. He died at Omega Cottage, Worthing, on 16th September 1851 and was buried at Gravesend in a handsome tomb in the form of an obelisk surmounted by an urn. The Gravesend and Southend theatres were sold by his executors. His widow seems to have retained the Worthing theatre in her ownership as a matter of sentiment, and it was not sold until 1856, after her death. It had ceased to operate as a theatre in 1855 and became a wholesale grocery store. It survived until 1970, when both the theatre and Omega Cottage, which had been much altered, were demolished in order that the whole area surrounding them might be developed, despite the fact that the theatre has been listed as a building of special architectural or historic interest. But the fittings from the small circular library in the Cottage were salvaged and have been incorporated in the Worthing Museum as part of the Museum's display of period costumes.

The next thirty years after Thomas Trotter ended his lease was a period of unease in the history of the Brighton theatre. Theatrical life still had not acquired respectability, and this was reflected in what took place in Brighton. Trotter's immediate successor as lessee was John Brunton Junior, the son the John Brunton who had been the first tenant of the New Road building in 1807. He was born in 1775 and made his debut on the stage at Lincoln in 1793. He then joined his father's Norwich circuit and graduated to Covent Garden Theatre in 1800. Four years later he returned to the provinces, where he managed several theatres. On taking up the Brighton theatre new scenery for it was designed by his son, Richard Brunton. But the venture was not a success, and John Brunton was forced to close the theatre in November 1820. The scenery, wardrobe and properties, which had cost £2,000 to make, were sold for £66 19s. 0d. John Brunton did not immediately disappear from the scene as in the following year he acted as stage manager for the new lessee of the theatre. But he eventually moved on and in due course became the Manager of the West London theatre. He died in 1848. Two of his sisters, Louisa and Mary (Mrs Merry) were also on the stage but never seem to have appeared at the Brighton theatre. Mary was the better known in the profession, but Louisa perhaps made more sensation by marrying the first Earl of Craven in 1807.

For the single year of 1821 the Manager was someone of the name of Masters. In the next year he was succeeded by James Russell of 37 Regent Place, who had been stage manager at Drury Lane theatre. He lasted until 1830. Two events of interest occurred during his management, both in 1823, when the season lasted until April. On January 7th the first pantomime to be staged in Brighton, *Harlequin Versus Shakespeare or Christmas Gambols* was performed. Fifty to seventy years later the pantomime was to become perhaps the most rewarding feature of the theatrical year in Brighton. The other event was an example of the low status which both the journalistic and theatrical professions then enjoyed in the world. In September the critic of the *Brighton Gazette* named Levi Emmanuel Cohen so slated a performance of the stock company in *As You Like It* that when two actors in the company named Larkin and Chapman met Cohen in North Street they insulted him publicly. Whereupon he took them before the magistrates, who bound them over to keep the peace.

The next Manager and lessee after James Russell was an actor named Frederick Vining, who was responsible for the seasons of 1831 to 1838. During this period of the twenties and thirties Edmund Kean continued to make frequent appearances at the theatre in all his most famous roles. When in Brighton he used to stay at the Regent Hotel, which was then the building at the north-west corner of New Road and Church Street, afterwards for so long Crabb's wineshop (No. 30 New Road). Edmund Kean died in 1833. Thereafter his son, Charles Kean, sometimes took his place. Others who appeared in Brighton at this time were Eliza Vestris or Madame Vestris as she was called, Charles and Fanny Kemble, William Charles Macready and the singer, Madame Sala, mother of the well-known journalist, George Augustus Sala, who lived at No. 2 Eastern Terrace later in the century.

The thirties also saw the debut in Brighton of two players who were to become very famous in the next decade. The first was Helena Faucit Saville who acted under the name of Helen Faucit. On 29th December 1833 she opened in Brighton as Juliet in *Romeo and Juliet*. Five years later her appearance at Covent Garden Theatre made her a national star and she really succeeded to the position occupied for so short a time by Fanny Kemble. She acted several times in Paris and on 16th January played Ophelia before King Louis-Philippe at the Tuileries. She seems to have retained some residential connection with Brighton as on 25th August 1851 she was married in St Nicholas's Church, Brighton, to Theodore Martin, the second son of James Martin of Edinburgh, whom she had met in Edinburgh when acting in his translation of the French play *King René's Daughter*. She continued acting in London until 1866 and in the provinces until 1879.

After the Prince Consort's death in 1861 Theodore Martin was chosen by Queen Victoria to write the Prince's life and in 1880, after the concluding volume had appeared, he was made a Knight Commander of the Bath. Through her husband's connection with the Queen, Lady Martin, as she became, often gave command performances or recitations at Windsor Castle. She died in 1898 and the *Dictionary of National Biography* called her 'the greatest interpreter of the poetical drama that living memory can recall'. An alto relievo profile in marble of her was placed by her husband in the church of Llantysilio in Wales, near to his estate of Bryn-tysilio, and a replica of this was given to the original Shakespeare Memorial Theatre at Stratford-on-Avon. A marble pulpit, designed by G. F. Bodley, was also erected to her memory in Stratford church.

The second figure who first made his appearance in Brighton in the eighteen-thirities was Dion Boucicault. He first took the stage name of Lee Morton and appeared as Sir Giles Overreach in *A New Way to Pay Old Debts* on 30th July 1838. Later, when he became successful in London, he acted under his own name, except that this was originally spelled Boursiquot. But he was perhaps better known in his own life as a dramatist — one of the most prolific of the century. Most of his plays are now largely forgotten. He frequently acted in Brighton during the next twenty-five years in both his own and other plays. In 1876 he retired to America where, according to the *Dictionary of National Biography*, he repudiated his wife, Agnes Robertson, and made 'other so-called nuptial arrangements, casting on his children an unmerited stigma'. He died there in 1890. His son of the same name married Irene Vanbrugh.

The theatrical performances of those days were marathon affairs and lasted at least four hours. Usually three plays were given. The first two of these were intended for the occupants of the stalls and boxes, who had paid the full price for their seats. The third play was usually a farce, intended for the occupants of the gallery, who were admitted for half-price after 9 o'clock. They sometimes rushed in like a torrent, whistling and shouting, while some of 'the quality' took the opportunity to retire at this moment.

One of the plays most often performed at this period was *Speed the Plough* by Thomas Morton. This is now quite forgotten except for one of its non-characters. All through the play the characters keep asking each other 'What will Mrs Grundy say?' Mrs Grundy was a neighbour but she never appears in the play. Her name and question have passed into the English language.

In addition to straight plays at the Theatre Royal, Brighton, an opera company sometimes made a visit at this period and occasionally even a circus. Slightly later — 4th and 6th November 1845 — Marie Taglioni danced in the theatre in *Les Sylparbes* and *Nathalic*. Some amateur dramatic performances were also given. In 1835 the Brighton Amateur Dramatic Society, which had been founded in 1827, acted in *Love and Reason* and *The Miller and His Men* by Isaac Pocock for the benefit of the Sussex County Hospital. One of the most curious amateurs to tread the boards was Barnard Gregory. He was a jack of all trades who at one time or other was a banker, chemist, wine merchant, property speculator, insurance broker, newspaper editor, newspaper proprietor and actor. In 1824 he built St Margaret's Church, Canon Place, Brighton, as a financial speculation following the construction of Regency Square. He then became editor of *The Brighton Gazette*. During the season of 1827 he was allowed to play the parts of Shylock, King Lear, Othello, Macbeth and Falstaff in the Brighton theatre. The perfomances seem to have passed off without protest. But he later acquired the ownership of a scurrilous paper named *The Satirist* which libelled so many people that, when he appeared on the London stage, the people whom he had attacked attended in force and hissed him off the stage. He was in fact forced to give up acting. But he again tackled Othello and Richard III in Brighton in 1841.

During the eighteen-thirties, though the Court came to Brighton every season, King William IV and Queen Adelaide seem not to have patronised the theatre. But on 13th January 1836 the King's sister, Princess Augusta, attended a performance of *Wild Oats* by John O'Keefe in which Helen Faucit played the pretty Quakeress.

Frederick Vining's management of 1831 to 1838 was followed by a period of misfortune. Charles Hill, who assumed management in 1839, fell into financial difficulties and decamped to New York in 1840. His successors, E. T. Holmes and C. Walton, lasted for only the single season of 1840. The next attempt by John Harroway and John Faucit Saville, the brother of the actress, Helen Faucit (Saville), in 1841 was more successful and, in their second season, they were able out of the proceeds to present to the Stewards of Brighton races a handsome silver cup with cover with an inscription on each side, valued at a hundred guineas. This was won outright in 1842 by Colonel Wyndham's horse Singleton. One wonders whether it is now still in existence and who owns it. Colonel Wyndham was probably a son of the third Earl of Egremont and brother of the first Lord Leconfield, both of Petworth House.

The next two Managers of the theatre lasted for two years each: Edward Hooper of No. 1 Castle Square, Brighton, who came from Bath, from 1844 to 1846 and Charles Poole from 1847 to 1849.

On 19th February 1845 Queen Victoria and Prince Albert, during their last visit to Brighton, attended a performance of *The Honey Moon* by John Tobin and *The Waterman*.

The winter of 1848–9 was perhaps the most brilliant season that Brighton has ever seen, when so many of those who had been driven from their countries by the revolution of 1848 found their way to this fashionable English resort. One feature of the season was the appearance at the theatre for the whole week of 1st November 1848 of Jenny Lind and Frederick Lablache. They sang in *La Somnambula* by Bellini and *La Figlia del Regimento* by Donizetti. The conductor of the company was no less a person than Michael Balfe, who was the composer of *The Bohemian Girl* and of other operas which had great popularity in the late nineteenth century but are now forgotten. The price of admission was 10s. 6d. for the boxes, and 5s. 0d. for the gallery. The receipts were £1,952 10s. 6d., of which £1,635 19s. 0d. was paid for the eight artistes and £140 for the hire of the theatre, leaving a profit of £276 11s. 0d.

This, however, was a flash in the pan. George Belcour of Dublin and Edinburgh was the lessee for the single year of 1850. During the season of 1851 the theatre was closed.

The next lessee was Henry Farren of No. 13 Montpelier Road, who was the son of the better-known actor, William Farren. He put on a season of plays in 1852 and 1853. The latter ended disastrously on 28th February 1854. The plays announced were *The Lady of Lyons* by Edward Bulmer Lytton and *Jack Sheppard* by J. B. Buckstone. The house was well filled. But the curtain, which was due to rise at 7 p.m. went up half an hour late, when an announcement was made from the stage that Henry Farren was absent and his part would be taken by an understudy. The performance of the first play was perfunctory. A farce named *The Unprotected Female* seems to have been added to the bill. At midnight the performance of *Jack Sheppard* began without the overture, as the musicians had dispersed, not having been paid. At 2 a.m. the fifth act was still unfinished, when the actress, Louisa Howard, who was playing Jack, came forward and announced that the scene-shifters were on strike through not having been paid. What little money there was had been distributed amongst them and the musicians before they departed. The lights gradually failed through the diminution of the supply of gas, and the audience slowly dispersed.

Farren in fact owed debts amounting to £468. A writ had been issued against him by his dresser named Scriven. On the departure of the orchestra Farren, who was a violinist as well as an actor, attempted to lead the orchestra. But when a bailiff appeared in the theatre he escaped to the machine-pit and passed through the trap to the roof, whence he was lowered by ropes into New Road, He made his way to the house of a friend named Charles Phillips who had a stationer's and printer's business at the top of West Street. There he spent the night. Meanwhile another member of the troupe named Fred Morton, who resembled Farren in appearance, was arrested in his place as he left the stage door. By the time that Morton was able to prove his identity Farren was beyond reach. The next morning he had left by train from Hove station for Portsmouth, whence he made his way in due course to New York. He died in St Louis, where he had taken charge of a theatre, in 1860 aged only 37. He was declared bankrupt in England. But by some hitherto unsuspected assets having eventually been declared to the court, his liabilities seem to have been discharged in full, as late as 1877.

Following the disappearance of Henry Farren the Brighton theatre was advertised as to let. From this position of uncertainty it was rescued by one of the important figures in the theatre's history, Henry John Nye Chart.

CHAPTER III

HENRY JOHN NYE CHART AND THE SECOND THEATRE IN NEW ROAD, 1854—1876.

HENRY JOHN CHART, to give him his correct name, was born in London on 27th October 1821. Porter's *History of the Theatres of Brighton* says that the birth occurred in Dean Street, Soho. He was in fact baptised at St Anne's Church, Soho on 3rd January 1822. His parents were John and Elizabeth Maria Chart. The father was a tailor of St Marylebone. Henry John was the eldest of a family of three sons and two daughters. With the family lived a cabinet-maker named Henry Nye, who was an enthusiastic and talented amateur actor and who was to have a considerable influence on Henry John Chart's career.

The real home of the Charts was at Newdigate in Surrey. The parish registers there at this period contain a number of entries relating to the family. Most of the men were also tailors. A later child of John and Elizabeth Chart named Angelina was baptised at Newdigate in 1824. Members of the family remained resident there for the next fifty years. A John Chart was Churchwarden in 1877, when the parish church was restored.

Henry John Chart was apprenticed to the piano manufacturers, Broadwood and Sons. The *Brighton Herald*, in its obituary of him, says that one of the partners in this firm had an estate near Rusper, which adjoined the parish of Newdigate on the south in the neighbouring county of Sussex. The young man at first worked in the tuning section of the firm. While in this occupation he followed his friend Henry Nye's example in taking up amateur acting and played with the City Histrionic Theatre Company. He did not like the piano business and in 1840, against his father's wishes, left it to become a professional actor. As a stage name he adopted that of his friend, Henry Nye, but later modified this to Henry Nye Chart. His first engagement was at the Ryde theatre in the Isle of Wight. For some time he must have lived the precarious life of a provincial actor of those times. But he eventually attracted the attention of Samuel Phelps, who was then the Manager of the Sadlers Wells Theatre, and played for a while in that theatre.

He first made his way to Brighton in 1850. Throughout his life he was devoted to his father and brothers, and the move to Brighton may have been made because his father was then living there, at No. 29 Bond Street, though this is not clear. At the same time Henry Nye had established a cabinet-maker and upholstery business at No. 45 Market Street. Henry Chart joined George Belcour's Company for the season of 1850. The first roles which he played in the Brighton theatre were that of the Hunchback in *The Fathom* and the title role in *That Rascal Jack* on 31st August 1850.

During the season of 1851, when the Brighton theatre was closed, Henry Chart joined M. H. Simpson's company at the Theatre Royal, Glasgow, of which George Belcour was also a member, and later Mr Addison's company at Doncaster. In 1852, when the Brighton theatre re-opened, he accepted an engagement with Henry Farren as low comedian and stage-manager. Amongst the parts which he then played were Bob Acres in *The Rivals*, Tony Lumpkin in *She Stoops to Conquer*, Colonna in *The Corsican Brothers* by Dion Boucicault, Uncle Tom in *Uncle Tom's Cabin*, the first Grave-digger in *Hamlet*, Roderigo in *Othello*, Trinculo in *The Tempest* and Touchstone in *As You Like It*. The last two of these parts must have appealed to him particularly as visual records of his performances in them were made. His great-grandson, Mr D. P. Kindersley, has an engraving of a scene in *The Tempest*, showing him with the jester, Trinculo. As Touchstone Chart was modelled by the Brighton sculptor, Henry Pepper. At the time of Chart's death this figure or bust was said to be on view in the theatre but since then it has vanished. Chart had his first benefit performance on 15th December 1852. When Henry Farren failed in 1854. Henry Chart was amongst his debtors to the tune of £49 12s. 4d.

When the theatre was advertised as to let Henry Chart came forward as lessee and was accepted as such by the proprietor, George Cobb, who had succeeded his uncle, Hewitt Cobb. He was given a lease for three years at the rent of £400 a year. This lease was renewed on the same terms in 1857, 1860 and 1863. He also rented the cottage attached to the theatre for £20 a year and moved into this himself. He appointed Charles Phillips as his acting Manager and William Wheeler as the keeper of the box office. The latter retained that office until his death at the age of 75 in 1875, when he was succeeded by his grandson, William Weeton Wheeler. The leader of the orchestra until 1872 was Leopold Stern.

Chart opened his first season at the theatre on 29th July 1854 with *The Bachelor of Arts* by Pelham Hardwicke and a fairy extravaganza entitled *Open Sesame!* in which he played the part Hassarac. In his opening address he said:

'Like Napier in the Baltic we must
By discipline and practice quickly do
All that becomes a willing crew.'

Chart's first alteration to the interior of the theatre was to add backs to the benches in the pit and to remove the royal box from the circle. Queen Victoria had not visited Brighton since 1845, and the Royal Pavilion had been sold to the Town Commissioners in 1850.

Henceforward Chart's professional name became Nye Chart. He formed his own stock company, as it was then called, which would now be known as a repertory company. The principal actor in it was Robert Soutar. The Treasurer was his father, John Chart, who had presumably by this time become reconciled to his son's career on the stage. John Chart occasionally had his own benefit performance. He held the position of Treasurer until his death in 1836. He was succeeded in it by his second son, Thomas Rentle Chart, who was unmarried and lived with his older brother, Henry John Nye Chart. He died in 1875, when the place was taken by the third son, Frederick Bishop Chart.

Throughout each season for the next twelve years Henry John Nye Chart's company presented a mixed programme of contemporary and classical plays, interspersed with visits from London stars such as Charles Kean, Charles James Mathews (the son of Charles Mathews) who had married Madame Vestris, Madame Celeste (or Celine Celeste-Elliott) and Madame Adelaide Ristori, frequent performances by amateurs and occasional visits by opera companies. Amongst the amateurs who appeared at this time was one of the sons of Henry Nye, John Kent Nye, who became a well-known Brighton solicitor. Another of his sons, Thomas Nye, eventually graduated to the professional stage. In July 1855 Nye Chart's company also appeared at the Theatre Royal, Worthing, shortly before that theatre finally closed.

On the occasion of the marriage of the Princess Royal to the Crown Prince of Prussia on 25th January 1858 the theatre put on the appropriately-named play *Bridal Morn; or the Happies Day of My Life*. This was followed, first by *Our Wife; or the Rose of Amiens*, then by a farcical interlude called *Eight Hours at the Seaside* including two new scenes *The Queen's Road near the Terminus* and *A Scene on Brighton Beach* and finally by the 'screaming farce' called *Slasher and Crasher*.

In August of that year a play-bill announced the appearance for three nights of 'the distinguished and celebrated comedian, Sir William Don, Bart.' One does not know whether this baronet was a genuine article and therefore a most unusual bird to find on the stage at the time, or whether he belonged to the same category as Lord George Sanger later in the century whose title was self-endowed. One of the plays in which Sir William Don appeared was *Box and Cox*. This was not the operetta by Sir Arthur Sullivan and F. C. Burnand but the earlier farce of the same name by Maddison Morton.

A year later another bill announced the appearance at the theatre of 'the great Elizabethan rider, Varney, wonderful equestrian performances, great leaping act, through hoops, balloons, etc., on the wild horse of Bastroyket'.

A reference to the Theatre Royal in a local guide-book published in 1860 shows how far the theatre still had to go before it achieved complete respectability. This was *Brighton As It Is: Its Pleasures, Practices and Pastimes — with a Short Account of the Social and Inner Life of the Inhabitants, being a Complete Guide Book for Residents and Visitors* by 'A Graduate of the University of London'. This mentions 'all those evils which experience has proved to be incidental to amusements of this kind' (the theatre). There was a gin palace nearby, and therefore after 11 p.m. the colonnade was used by prostitutes as a promenade ground and 'presents a very animated appearance' when the theatrical performance ended.

But even this very special moralising guide-book did not suggest that the theatre itself was not respectably conducted during Henry John Nye Chart's management. Once again at this period it had royal patrons. On 17th April 1862 the old Duchess of Cambridge, who was the last surviving member of the Royal Family of George IV's generation, and her daughter, Princess Mary, who was later Duchess of Teck and the mother of Queen Mary, attended an amateur performance in aid of distressed Lancashire operatives. The three plays were *Pride of the Market* by J. R. Planché, *The Happy Man* and *Who Speaks First*. Madame Celeste appeared as Marton in the first of these. But the male characters were played by the officers of 9th Lancers. The prices were 7s. 6d. for the stalls, 5s. 0d. for the boxes, 2s. 6d. for the pit and slips and 1s. 0d. for the gallery. The usual admission at half-price in the interval was not available. On 10th March 1863, the day of the Prince of Wales's marriage to Princess Alexandra of Denmark, a special matinée performance of *Jeannie Deans* by Dion Boucicault was given to a 'fashionable and full audience'. [1]The prices were 2s. 6d. for the circle, 1s. 6d. for the boxes and 6d. for the gallery. At the evening performance on the same day the façade of the theatre was illuminated. The Duchess of Cambridge and Princess Mary must have had some special connection with the 9th Lancers as a year later, on 18th November 1863, they attended another of their productions, when the regiment staged *An Ugly Customer*, *Nothing Venture* and *More Blunders Than One*. Nine days later they saw a professional performance of *The First Night* and *Poor Nobleman!*, both by Afred Wigan.

An extremely badly-worded letter to Henry Nye Chart from Charles Dickens has survived from this period and is now framed in the stalls bar of the theatre together with a handbill of the plays to which the letter refers. These were *The Wonder! A Woman Keeps a Secret*, an old three act comedy of 1676 by Mrs Centlivre; a farce named *A Kiss in the Dark* by J. B. Buckstone; and a new play described as a burlesque called *Esmeralda and the Sensation Goat*. Nye Chart played the lead in all three plays. The letter was written

[1] Porter's *History of the Theatres of Brighton*.

from Tavistock House on 28th March 1863 and began 'My dear Chart, Just a line to let you know that we got back safe from our Brighton trip and I must say that we greatly enjoyed ourselves. I think that you did your part first class. You are Lissardo (Chart's part in *The Wonder)* at heart. The Theatre Royal is not a bad place and well patronised I shall certainly visit it again when I am down there. I am hoping to see you when in Town next week to fix up when and where.' No doubt Dickens did attend the theatre again on one of his many visits to Brighton, which he liked so much, but we have no record of this.

In all that was written about Henry Nye Chart both during his life and after his death it stands out that, like Thomas Trotter before him, he was a man of principle, which was then very rare in the still relatively disreputable world of the theatre or, as the *Brighton Herald*[1] wrote in his obituary, he never allowed a member of his company to know the want of his salary'. It is evident also that he was a man of ability as it was not easy at that period to make a stock company prosper. This they eventually did, and by 1866 Nye Chart was ready to consider a more ambitious project.

Since 1807 the theatre had been in the ownership in half-shares of Hewitt Cobb and Sir Thomas Clarges. Cobb died on 21st January 1822 and left the residue of his estate to his nephew, George, eldest son of his brother George Cobb Senior. Sir Thomas Clarges died in February 1834. His wife predeceased him, and his financial affairs seem to have been very involved. It was not until 1842 that anything was done about the Theatre Royal. By then his sole executor, Jonathan Brundrett, had also died. So the only survivor of Brundrett's executors, who was Sir Gregory Alnutt Lewin, sought the direction of the Court of Chancery on the subject. By order of the Master of the Rolls Clarges's half-share was sold by auction on 27th October 1842. It fetched £1,650 and was bought by George Cobb who already owned the other half-share, inherited from his uncle, Hewitt Cobb, in 1822.

George Cobb Junior had been born in 1787 and was an attorney of Clements Inn, though he may never have practised as such. He was a friend of J. M. W. Turner and is said to have drawn up Turner's will. If he did so, then he was involuntarily the cause of

[1] 29th June, 1876.

much contention and dissatisfaction even after the case was settled and Turner's pictures had been lodged in the National Gallery. Turner left Cobb his palette. This Cobb later gave to the Brighton marine artist, R. H. Nibbs, whose father had been a member of the orchestra at the Brighton Theatre Royal. Nibbs subsequently passed on the palette to the National Gallery. Cobb was also a Brighton Councillor and later an Alderman. He lived, at any rate at the end of his life, at No. 1 Hampton Terrace Brighton. He survived until 1877.

In 1866 Henry John Nye Chart was able to persuade George Cobb, who was then 79 years old, to sell the theatre to him, so that it could be enlarged and rebuilt. The purchase price was £7,500. Nye Chart himself could not produce a capital sum of this size. He therefore obtained the help of a syndicate which put up £5,500 of the money. Robert White of Bow Street, Covent Garden, London, subscribed £1,000; Robert Bacon, hotel keeper, and Ewen Evershed, solicitor, £300 each. Five other people provided £200 each and twenty-nine others £100 each. On the day after the date of his purchase, namely 8th May 1866, Nye Chart completed a deed of mortgage in favour of George Augustus Schneider, Heneage William Dering and William Langworthy as trustees in favour of the subscribers as a whole. The capital sum was to be repaid in equal instalments of £1,833 6s. 8d. on 8th May 1869, 1871 and 1873, with interest at 6% in the meanwhile. In actual fact these repayments were never made in Nye Chart's life, though the interest was punctually paid. It was not until eight years after his death that his widow repaid this capital. So on 6th June 1873 Robert White and George Augustus Oliver, the licensee of the Eagle Tavern, City Road, London, took over the whole burden of the mortgage, which was assigned to them by the trustees. At the same time the new mortgagees advanced a further sum of £500 to Nye Chart himself.

As soon as Nye Chart had completed the purchase of the theatre he proceeded to embark upon rebuilding it. The architect whom he chose was Charles James Phipps (1835–1897). Mrs Odell in one of her books on the Theatre Royal at Worthing says that no theatres were built in England between 1840 and 1860. Covent Garden — perhaps the most magnificent theatre in the country —

was actually rebuilt in its present form in 1858. But broadly speaking her statement was true. It was a lean period for the theatre. The eighteen-sixties on the other hand were a prolific period of theatre-building. Phipps had largely a monopoly of these theatres. He was born in Bath in 1835 and, after being articled to Wilson and Fowler, set up in business there in 1857. He rebuilt the Theatre Royal at Bath in 1863 and the Theatre Royal at Nottingham in 1865. During his career he was responsible for designing theatres in Bristol, Plymouth, Torquay, Eastbourne, Swansea, Worcester, Portsmouth, Sheffield, South Shields, Darlington, Hastings, Leicester, Northampton, Leamington, Liverpool, Wolverhampton, Dover, Edinburgh, Glasgow, Dumfries, Aberdeen, Dublin, Belfast, Londonderry and Cork. He also entered the London field and designed no less than eleven theatres there between 1869 and his death in 1897. These were the Variety at Hoxton (1869); the Vaudeville (1870); Sadler's Wells (1897); the Princess's (1880); the interior of the Haymarket (1880, rebuilt again in 1904); the Savoy (1881); the London Palladium (1884, rebuilt in 1910); the Prince of Wales's (1886, rebuilt in 1937); the Strand (1887); the Lyric (1888); the Garrick, with Walter Emden for W. S. Gilbert, (1889); and Her Majesty's, with the Carlton Hotel adjoining (1895).

The old theatre in Brighton closed on 21st May 1866. A contract for £4,000 with Phipps was signed on 25th June. The contractor was David Bland of London and the Clerk of Works G. R. Tasker. The work was completed in just under four months. Of the exterior the colonnade was left untouched, except that a statue of one of the muses carrying a torch was added above it. On the first floor a central projection was built out which Porter calls a conservatory. This probably served as the first bar for the dress circle. It was lit by three tall, round-headed windows facing east and one in each return front. The flanking windows on the main building were altered to match these, taking in the former recesses above. In the centre of the parapet of this conservatory or projection was a handsome Royal cartouche.

Above the old building was added an unwieldy and out-of-proportion top hamper with an eaves bracket cornice. This contained the new gallery. On the stuccoed surface of the east front

Plate 3.

New Road in 1876, showing the Theatre after the rebuilding of 1866.

(Reproduced by kind permission of Mr. D. P. Kindersley.)

the single word 'Theatre' was written, but on the new north front above the adjoining houses, Nos 13–15 New Road, were the words 'New Theatre Royal and Opera House'.

The entrance was in the centre of the east elevation, through what came later to be the bar of the pit, now the back stalls bar. But it did not lead straight into the auditorium. The way in was by means of a corridor to the left or south. Out of this corridor a curved staircase, which was probably the original staircase of the 1806–7 theatre, led to the dress circle. This still survives but is now a subsidiary staircase used for exit only. Entrance to the upper galleries was, as it is now, by a separate staircase entered from the colonnade further north.

The auditorium was of the horseshoe shape which was then normal for a Victorian theatre, but slightly less splayed at the stage end than it is now. On each side of the stage was one box on three levels flanked by giant twin pilasters with leaf capitals. Eight other smaller boxes were placed behind the dress circle, four more or less at the angles immediately behind the stage boxes and four at the back. The four back ones were removed in 1912. In addition to the two existing galleries a third circle known as the gallery was added, of which the lowest portion was called the amphitheatre. The ceiling of the theatre was ribbed with a pattern of fan ornamentation in blue and gold surrounding the central chandelier. Below this was a narrow frieze of Greek mythological figures, with larger sculptured figures over the proscenium and boxes. The fronts of the galleries were treated in imitation of marble and coloured azure, red and chocloate. The lobbies, corridors and staircases were coloured green. Elsewhere the prevailing tints were warm purple, cream and light buff. This decoration was the work of Green and King of Baker Street, London. The stalls had patent folding seats designed by C. J. Phipps and made by Wadman of Bath. The act-drop was a capriccio of an Italian sixteenth century water-party in which a magnificent canopied barge awaits its passengers at the quay of a luxurious classical villa, while other fancy vessels laden with people have already pulled away into the main stream of the river or lake. This was painted by George Gordon of Bristol and the figures by W. Harford. In 1886 it was in the possession of Henry Saunders of the Blacksmiths

Plate 4.
Elevation of The Theatre of 1866.
Photograph taken during the week of the 6th November 1882.
(Reproduced by kind permission of Mr. Philippe Garner.)

Plate 5.
Interior of the Theatre in 1876.
Painting by I. S. Lenox.
(Reproduced by kind permission of Mr D. P. Kindersley.)

Arms Inn, North Street. A copy of it has survived and can be seen in the stalls bar of the theatre.

If the auditorium of today is compared with that of 1866 the main fabric of the galleries, supported on slender columns, and the stage boxes are identical. But of the original decor virtually all that survives comprises the pilasters flanking the boxes and the central chandelier in the ceiling. Everything else was refurbished in the later redecorations, particularly that of 1927. The accommodation of the theatre was increased by the rebuilding from 1,200 to 1,900.

The Manager's house or cottage at the north-west corner of the theatre site was converted into dressing-rooms with two green rooms. The stage door giving access to them was approached by a long passage or twitten between the main auditorium and No. 13 New Road, as the present stage door in Bond Street was not instituted until 1894. This passage still exists but is not used. At the inner entrance was a tiny lodge for the stage door-keeper with an equally miniscule office over it, where Mrs Nye Chart later held court.

As Henry Nye Chart lost his home as the result of the rebuilding he installed himself in the nearest house to the theatre that he could find. The theatre itself occupied No 11 and 12 New Road. The adjoining building on the south, No. 10, was then, as now, the Colonnade Hotel. He therefore rented No. 9. This stood between the Colonnade Hotel and the first of the shops (No. 7) which was occupied by the gun-smiths, C. and H. Weston, for nearly a hundred years. (There seems never to have been a No. 8 New Road.) Nye Chart must evidently have had a short lease of the house at first, but on 5th April 1870 he obtained a lease for forty years at the rent of £76 a year. Seven years after his death his widow purchased the freehold of the house for £1,800. No. 9 was uniform with the other houses in New Road which had been built about 1820, with a colonnade on the ground floor and a deeply projecting bow window above this. But behind the colonnade in front of the house was a covered way which lead to stables, originally known as Castle Stables and later as Pavilion Hunting Stables. On 29th September 1867 Nye Chart took over the remainder of the lease of these stables for twenty-one years from 25th March 1851 at the rent of £36 a year. He converted them into

Plate 6.

The stage back-drop in the theatre of 1866, painted by George Gordon and W. Halford.

(Reproduced by kind permission of the Directors of Brighton Theatre Royal Limited.)

property rooms and storage space for scenery. This was enclosed fronting New Road by two large gates which were fastened only by a simple catch in order to allow egress from the stage in case of fire. No. 9 New Road remained Chart's home until his death in 1876 and his widow's home after him until her death. It was incorporated into the theatre as part of the alterations of 1894.

The first season in the rebuilt theatre opened on 15th October 1866 with a performance of *Society* by Tom Robertson, followed by a burlesque called *Lucia di Lammermoor*. After the singing of *God Save the Queen* en masse Nye Chart declaimed a long prologue written by William Sawyer, beginning:

'With pleasure undisguised and honest pride,
That quite in vain I should attempt to hide
(For still the heart speaks in the lips despite),
I bid *you* welcome in *my* house tonight.
My house, forgive, if with too high a tone,
I speak of what I've sought so long to own;
And looking round say, is it, "Yes" or "No",
A house a man may well feel proud to show.
We've heard enough in prose, too much in rhymes,
About those very wonderful old times;
Indeed some people take so great a pride in 'em,
One's apt to wish that they had liv'd and died in 'em.
But, for my part, I know no far or near age
That would appear superior to this *pier-age*'.

(The West Pier had only been opened nine days previously.)

He went on to mention some of the people who had been responsible for the different kinds of work in the theatre:

'There's Phipps,[1] so clever, affable and Bland,[2]
Who's well accomplished all his leader planned.
Green too and King[3] deserve congratulations
Upon the beauty of their decorations;
And in this act-drop Gordon[4] has delighted us
With the sweet scene to which he has invited us.
For just one more I must approval ask

[1] The architect.
[2] The contractor.
[3] The decorators.
[4] The painter of the drop-scene.

Bravely our Tasker[1] has got through his task.

The play ran until 21st October.

In the following year another event occurred which was important both to the career of Henry Nye Chart and to the history of the Theatre Royal. On 27th July 1867 he married Ellen Elizabeth Rollason, who had been a member of his company for about two years. After her marriage she continued to act but also assumed responsibility for the control of events behind the curtain. For the next ten years Henry Nye Chart continued to own and manage the theatre, as before with a stock company. John Kent Nye, although an amateur frequently played with the company on a seemingly professional basis. But whole amateur companies also performed from time to time. As before, leading actors from London made occasional visits and sometimes an opera company was heard. Charles James Mathews and Dion Boucicault were amongst the stars who continued to make appearances. New names were Charles Fechter, Samuel Phelps, J. L. Toole, Barry Sullivan and Amy Sedgwick.

The last two of these had a more substantial connection with Brighton or its district than was provided by acting. In 1886 when Barry Sullivan left the stage he retired to No. 45 Albany Villas, Hove, and lived there until his death in 1891. Amy Sedgwick was married on 15th October 1858 in St. Michael's Church, Southwick, Sussex. Her husband was Dr W. B. Parkes, a London physician and brother of the Reverend Frank Parkes, who was Vicar of Southwick parish. Dr Parkes died in 1863, and his wife temporarily gave up the stage. But after two years she returned to it and, like Helen Faucit, frequently gave dramatic readings before the Queen. In 1873 she married again and once more retired from the stage. Her last performances on this occasion were actually in Brighton on 3rd to 7th March in *The Lady of Lyons* by Edward Bulmer-Lytton, in *The Love Chase* and *The Hunchback*, both by Sheridan Knowles, in *The Unequal Match* by Tom Taylor and in *Masks and Faces* by Charles Reade and Tom Taylor. Then on 27th May she married at St Andrew's Old Church, Hove, Charles Pemberton, a well-known Liverpool solicitor. She was given away by Sir John Cordy Burrows, who had been Mayor of

[1] The Clerk of the Works.

Brighton in 1857 and 1858 and was to be again in 1872. Her second husband lived only two years. After his death she again returned to the stage but once more retired from it on her third marriage in 1878 to Charles Goostry. But she still made occasional dramatic readings by royal command at Osborne. She died in 1897.

On 11th November 1870 the old Duchess of Cambridge made another appearance at the theatre for a performance of *Secret Service* and *A Bachelor of Arts*.

During 1872 Henry John Nye Chart had a serious illness but recovered from it successfully and re-appeared on the stage in August. On 19th August 1875 he lost his brother, Thomas Rentle Chart, through dropsy at the age of only 43. He was much affected by this loss but was otherwise in good health and intended to go to Paris on holiday on 31st May 1876. But a few days previously, while on a picnic at Patcham — then a rustic village — he suffered the re-occurrence of a nasal haemorrhage, by which he had been affected a few years previously. He never recovered from this, seems to have developed a 'affection of the heart'[1] and died at No. 9 New Road on 17th June 1876 aged 55. He was buried in his brother's grave in the Brighton and Preston Cemetery on 22nd June. His was not a long-lived family as his remaining brother, Frederick Bishop Chart, was only 50 when he died on 19th July 1878. He was also buried in the same grave.

In July 1877 Ellen Nye Chart erected to the memory of her husband a stained glass window in the parish church of St Peter's, Newdigate, which was the original home of his family and where she and her husband had spent their honeymooon. The church was being restored at the time and a south aisle added to the nave. One of the Churchwardens was a John Chart, who held this office for forty-six years until his death in 1878. He has been called Henry John Chart's uncle, but as the name of the latter's father was also John it is unlikely that two surviving brothers would have had the same Christian name. So more probably the Churchwarden, John Chart, was a cousin of an older generation. The window was placed in the centre of the new south aisle. It is of good design for 1877 and shows Christ surrounded by women and children with the text 'Suffer little children to come unto me and forbid

[1] *Brighton Gazette*, 22nd June, 1876.

them not, for of such is the kingdom of Heaven'. Underneath is the inscription 'In loving memory of the late Henry John Chart of Brighton presented by his widow, 1877.'

Henry John Nye Chart's will had been made about seven months before his death. It was dated 24th November 1875. The executors were his friends John Kent Nye and Daniel Harding Greenin of No. 20 East Street, Brighton, toy-dealer. He left everything to his wife without qualification as to her remarriage. But his estate was valued at under £1,500 on account of the outstanding mortgage on the Theatre Royal.

Of Henry Nye Chart as an actor it was said that 'he belonged to the happy medium of comedians'[1] not of the first class. His contribution to the stage was much more as a manager than as an actor. His three main assets seem to have been honesty, kindness of heart and great zeal. The *Brighton Gazette* in its obituary of him implied that he had been beset by financial difficulties for at least three seasons but had well overcome them by the time of his death and was looking forward to a prosperous future. His period of management came just at the time when the theatre in general was beginning to become respectable.

His achievement was to transform the Brighton theatre from a playhouse of little repute (save in the time of Thomas Trotter) into a respected local institution. His widow was able to build on these foundations and, during the sixteen years of her control of the Theatre Royal, to give it a national standing.

[1] *Brighton Gazette*, 22nd June, 1876.

Plate 7.
Henry John Nye Chart shortly before his death in 1876.
(Reproduced by kind permission of Mr. D. P. Kindersley.)

CHAPTER IV

ELLEN ELIZABETH NYE CHART AND THE THEATRE ROYAL LIMITED, 1876—1892.

ONE CANNOT be precise about the date of birth of Ellen Elizabeth Rollason, or Nellie Rollason as she was usually called. According to her obituaries and her tombstone she was 51 when she died in 1892. This would mean that she was born in 1841. But there is no entry for the registration of her birth between 1837, when the registration of births was made compulsory, and 1842. One would therefore incline to think that her age was wrongly given out of actress's vanity. She was almost certainly born at Islington, but a search of the baptism registers for three parishes in Islington from 1831 to 1842 has revealed no entry for the name of Ellen Elizabeth Rollason. Her father, John Rollason, was a builder. She is said to have made her first appearance on the stage as a child in pantomimes and then to have achieved some success in London and the provinces. But we have no details of this until she came to Brighton in 1865. By this time she was an established actress and joined Henry Nye Chart's company to play leading roles.

Her first appearance in Brighton, in the original Theatre Royal in New Road, was on 29th July 1865, when she played the part of Pauline in *The Lady of Lyons* — an old play which had been in the repertoire of successive Brighton companies for many years. The first of her original creations was the role of Lucy in *The Counterfeit* by David Fisher, which had its first performance on any stage on 9th October 1865. Another success was as Violante in *The Wonder*.

When the second theatre in New Road was inaugurated on 15th October 1866 Nelly Rollason played the leading part of Maude Hetherington in Tom Robertson's comedy *Society*. Her last appearance before her marriage was as Jane Sternbold in *Still Waters Run Deep* by Tom Taylor on 9th July 1867.

After two years of acting together Nelly Rollason and Henry Nye Chart were married at St Mary's Church, Islington, on 27th July 1867. Their honeymoon was spent at Croydon and Newdigate. They returned to live at No. 9 New Road, Brighton, which by this time was known as Royal House. Here their only child, John Nye Chart II, was born on 30th April 1868. At the age of ten months he made his first appearance on the stage, being carried on as a baby in a play called *The Old Post Boy*. In due course he became a professional actor.

After her marriage Ellen Nye Chart assumed responsibility for the control of events behind the curtain, as well as continuing to act with the company. The first occasion when she and Henry Nye Chart appeared on the stage as man and wife was on 3rd August 1867 in *A Bird in the Hand Worth Two in the Bush*, when they were called before the curtain and given an ovation. At her first benefit on 24th February 1868 she played Mrs Henry Dove in *Married Life* by J. B. Buckstone. Other plays in which she had successes were as Beatrice in *Much Ado About Nothing*, as Lady Teazle in *School for Scandal*, as Kate Hardcastle in *She Stoops to Conquer*, as Adrienne Lecouvreur in *The Reigning Favourite* by John Oxenford, in *The Flying Scud*, *The Octoroon*, *The Coleen Bawn* and *Don Caesar de Bazan*, all by Dion Boucicault and in other plays now largely unknown such as *Camill's Husband* by Watts Phillips, *The Overland Route* and *The Ticket of Leave Man*, both by Tom Taylor, *Lady Audley's Secret* by George Roberts, *Blow for Blow* by H. J. Byron and *The Old Toll House*. Her last appearance on the stage with her husband was on 10th April 1876 in *The Ladies' Battle* by Charles Reade.

Henry Nye Chart died on 18th June of that year. He left the Theatre Royal to his wife and she assumed sole management of it. The theatre was redecorated, and her first season opened on 31st July during race week, when the Gaiety Comany under the direction of Robert Soutar presented a triple bill: *Rip Van Winkle* by Dion Boucicault, *Sold Again* and *The Guilty Governess*. The leading roles were played by Emily Farren, who was Robert Soutar's wife, and Edward Royce. Several other companies followed which presented, amongst other plays, *Frou Frou*, translated from the French by G. J. Comyns Carr, and *East Lynne*, adapted by Alfred

Kempe from Mrs Henry Wood's novel.

At Christmas there was, as usual, a pantomime: *Jack in the Box*. But immediately preceding it, on 18th, 19th and 20th December 1876 three special performances were given as 'complimentary benefits' to Mrs Nye Chart. These were organised by three admirers of her late husband who, as far back as 1866, had acted as the original trustees of the mortgage of the theatre which Nye Chart had entered into when a syndicate had made him an advance to enable him to buy the building. These were George Augustus Schneider, Heneage William Dering and William Langworthy. The mortgage on the theatre was still in existence, though these three trustees had assigned their interest in it to two other mortgagees in 1873. G. A. Schneider may have had some connection with the Nye Chart's other great friend, J. K. Nye, as Schneider's place of business was Treacher's Royal Library, No. 170 North Street, and another member of the organising committee was named Harry Treacher. J. K. Nye later entered into partnership with someone called Treacher, and his firm then became Nye and Treacher. Treacher's library subsequently changed sides in North Street and for many years was carried on at No. 1 North Street, east of Hanningtons. The library went out of business only in 1924, when the premises were acquired by Hanningtons and reconstructed.

The three special performances of December 1876 were intended to be in memory of Henry John Nye Chart and as a tribute to the noble manner in which his widow had assumed his mantle and was carrying on the theatre so efficiently since his death. The plays chosen were *New Men and Old Acres* by Tom Taylor, *London Assurance* by Dion Boucicault and *The School for Scandal*. But each night's performance comprised the immense programme that was normal at the period. Following the main play on the first night Mrs Stirling told the story of *A Poor Stroller;* On the second night the comedy scenes from *The Hunchback* by Sheridan Knowles were played; and on the third night a curtain-raiser named *His Last Legs* by W. B. Bernard was given. All three evenings ended with a 'ballet divertissement by Mlle Tanzoni and the ladies of the corps de ballet'. It was at first announced that Samuel Phelps would take the part of Sir Peter Teazle in *The*

School for Scandal, but he was not able to appear at the last moment, and his place was taken by 'Mr Chippendale'. J. C. Buckstone, the son of the dramatist, J. B. Buckstone, appeared with him. The women stars were Helen Barry and Ada Cavendish. The price of the boxes was £2 2s. 0d., £1 11s. 6d. and £1 1s. 0d., the stalls 5s. 0d., dress circle 4s. 0d., the pit stalls 3s. 0d., the upper circle 2s. 6d., the pit 1s. 6d., and the gallery 6d. As the result of the performances the trustees were able to hand Mrs Nye Chart a cheque for £397 9s. 7d.

Contrary to the usual practice at benefit nights, Mrs Nye Chart herself did not take part in any of the plays. But at the end of each performance she appeared on the stage, accompanied by her son, who was then aged 8, to acknowledge the applause of the house. In April 1877 a very handsome album was presented to her by the organisers, recording every detail of these three performances. This contains photographs of the members of the Nye Chart family, all the actors and actresses who took part in the plays the corps de ballet, the orchestra, led by Ferdinand Kessler, the stage staff, the front staff and the organisers themselves, together with plans and photographs of the theatre, a balance sheet of the money raised and lengthy press cuttings of advance publicity and accounts of the plays. This album still exists and belongs to Mrs Nye Chart's great-grandson, Mr D. P. Kindersley.

In 1877 following the pantomime, the stock company seems to have resumed work at the theatre. Mrs Chart herself appeared on the stage on 29th October 1877 for the first time since her husband's death, when she played Lady Franklin in *Money* by Edward Bulmer-Lytton on the occasion of her benefit. Henceforward the season was extended to cover the whole year. Visiting companies came more often to the theatre, instead of just visiting stars playing with the stock company. Amongst the famous names were J. L. Toole, Wilson Barrett, John Hare, Charles Wyndham, his wife Mary Moore, Lily Langtry, William and Madge Kendal. Madge Robertson, to give her her maiden name, was the youngest of a very large family of which was the eldest was the dramatist, Tom Robertson 1829-71, who wrote *Caste*. She was born in 1848 and lived until 1935. In her eighties, as Dame Madge Kendal, she made several appearances in Brighton, not on the stage but opening bazaars for a fee. She wore extravagantly antediluvian clothes and delighted in giving her opinion of 'the modern girl'.

Henry Irving made his first appearances in Brighton on 17th to 22nd December 1877 with three plays. These were *Hamlet, Charles I* by W. G. Wills and *The Bells,* with which he had made his first sensation in London in 1871. This play was an English version by Leopold Lewis of *Le Juif Polonais* by Erckmann and Chatrian. Ellen Nye Chart made her last appearances on the stage on 7th, 8th and 9th April 1879. Two nights had been announced for her benefit, but such was the competition for seats that a third night had to be added. She appeared as Helen in the old play *The Hunchback* and as Miami in the second act of *The Green Bushes* by J. B. Buckstone. Following *The Hunchback* J. L. Toole appeared as Spriggins in *Ici on Parle Français* or *French Before Breakfast* by T. J. Williams. On the second night Irving recited Bulwer Lytton's *Dream of Eugene Aram* which was his most spectacular recitation. He did not play in Brighton again until 1900.

From 1879 onwards the stock company seems to have faded out and was replaced by a touring company each week. One of these companies gave here on 19th September 1880 the first performance in England of the opera *La Mascotte* by Edmund Audran. The first performance in Brighton of a Gilbert and Sullivan opera, *H.M.S. Pinafore,* occurred in 1878, but not by the D'Oyly Carte Opera Company. *The Pirates of Penzance* followed in 1881; *Patience* in 1883 and *Princess Ida* in 1884. The first visit by the D'Oyly Carte Opera Company was with *Iolanthe* in 1883. For some years their appearance was with a single opera for a whole week, but in 1891 they brought for the first time several operas: *The Mikado, The Yeomen of the Guard* and *The Gondoliers.* But as long as the original Gilbert and Sullivan productions were still running at the Savoy Theatre, London — and the last of these, *The Grand Duke,* was not produced till 1896 — the visiting company was necessarily only a 'second eleven'.

The Carl Rosa Opera Company, which had been formed in 1875, seems not to have made an appearance in Brighton until 1889, when they brought a single opera *Paul Jones* by Robert Planquette. The *Brighton Herald* described this as a 'not unworthy successor of *Les Cloches de Corneville* and *Rip Van Winkle*' by the same composer. But it seems to have followed the latter into obscurity, rather than the former into reoccurring performances. The Carl Rosa seems not to have embarked on their monumental tours of several operas, or at least not to have brought them to Brighton, until 1896, when they performed *Hansel and Gretel*, *Tannhauser*, *Lohengrin*, *The Flying Dutchman*, *Carmen* and *Mignon* by Ambroise Thomas in a single week. At the same period there were visits to the Brighton theatre from the Italian Opera Company from Covent Garden with *Carmen*, *Faust*, *Il Trovatore* and *Lucia di Lammermoor*, while the English Opera Company brought almost the only English operas between Purcell and Britten to achieve a place in opera repertoire: *Maritana* by William Wallace, *The Bohemian Girl* by Michael Balfe, as well as the latter's less well known *The Rose of Castille*.

During the week of 11th April 1887 two operettas were performed: *The Beggar Student* by Millecer and *Dorothy* with words by B. C. Stephenson and music by Alfred Cellier. All that is notable about this programme is that the leading roles in *Dorothy* were taken by Hayden Coffin and Marie Tempest. The latter in fact made her name in this musical comedy. This was the first of numerous appearances on her part in Brighton, the last being in *Dear Octopus* in 1940.

In May 1887 Frank Benson brought his Shakespeare Company, which had been formed in 1883 to the Theatre Royal. They played in *Hamlet*, *Othello*, *Richard III*, *The Merchant of Venice* and *Much Ado About Nothing* as well as *The Corsican Brothers* by Dion Boucicault. This was the first of many visits to Brighton of the Benson Company which continued for at least the next thirty-five years. Sometimes they played in the theatre on one of the piers instead of at the Theatre Royal.

In 1883 matinée performances were inaugurated at the Brighton theatre, but not at first on fixed days of the week. These soon settled down to being on Thursdays and Saturdays. But not until well into the next century did the touring company of each week reckon to give more than a single matinée on the Saturday afternoon. Mrs. Nye Chart therefore improvised the arrangement of bringing a whole production from London, often with a star cast, to give a special matinée on Thursday afternoon. The timing for this must have needed very tricky arrangements. A performance begun at 2 p.m. can hardly have been over before about 4.45 p.m. There were two trains back to London between 5 and 6 o'clock. The second of these was a non-stop which left Brighton at 5.35 p.m. and arrived at Victoria at 6.45 p.m. A special coach must have been attached to the train for the scenery and costumes. Even if this were met by a horse-drawn van at Victoria and by cabs for the cast it must have been a tight squeeze to get the whole outfit back to the Haymarket or the Strand, in time for an evening performance at 8 p.m. The organisers must also have had more confidence in the punctuality shown by the London to Brighton and South Coast Railway than would now be possible in the case of British Railways.

This practice was followed from time to time by later managements, when such performances came to be called flying matinées. But the term was not used in Mrs Nye Chart's time. They were then called morning performances. In this way Brighton audiences saw (amongst other plays) an early performance of *The Private Secretary* by Charles Hawtrey; with W. S. Penly in the main role, on 19th May 1887; of *The Red Lamp* by Outram Tristram with Herbert Beerbohm Tree on 2nd June 1887, of the old play *Lady of Lyon* acted by Wilson Barrett on 5th April 1888 and of Tom Robertson's version of *David Garrick* acted by Charles Wyndham and Mary Moore on 15th November 1888. Perhaps the most remarkable of these flying matinées was the first occasion when a Brighton audience had an opportunity to see a play by Ibsen. *A Doll's House,* translated by William Archer, was the first of his plays to reach London. On 20th June 1889, within a fortnight of its being presented at the Novelty Theatre, it was brought to Brighton with Janet Achurch, William Waring and the whole cast.

Perhaps the institution for which Mrs Nye Chart was most famous comprised her annual Christmas pantomime, on the last night of which she always made a speech from the stage. These were extremely elaborate and modelled on the pantomimes for which the Drury Lane Theatre in London was famous at the time. But despite the expense involved they were also the most profitable feature of the season financially for the Brighton theatre and ran until the beginning of February each year.

The libretto and score of these pantomimes were published every year with illustrations of each scene and a list of the cast. One of these booklets has survived in the archives of the Theatre Royal. It actually dates from 1893, the year after Mrs Nye Chart's death, but is presumably typical of the earlier productions of her time. The title was *Aladdin or the Arabian Knight-Errant.* It was in twelve scenes, each of elaborate Chinese character. The scene 'Corridor in the Palace' (of the Chinese Emperor) was a very creditable composite imitation of rooms in the Royal Pavilion. Then followed the transformation scene 'From Winter to Summer', for which the Drury Lane pantomimes were celebrated, with a harlequinade and a 'budget of fun' comprising yet two more scenes.

The libretto was written by Henry John Nye Chart II who composed the work of several pantomimes at this period. It was written in rhyming couplets of exceptional banality such as:

'My nervous system's out of order latterly.
I'll go and get a drop of sal-volatile..'

It was full of Brighton allusions, for instance:

'I'll show you some sights, chock full of delights,
There's the Pier and the Royal Aquarium,
With fishes and pearls and bodyless girls.
The Skating Rink and Empire too we'll visit in turn.
To hear a concert at the Dome we eagerly yearn
Those organ recitals, which go through your vitals,
And promenade concerts we will not spurn.'

The melodies of the songs were interspersed in the text. These were popular songs of the time which were published with the permission of their publishers. The booklet had the usual quota of advertisements, particularly of Muratti's cigarettes. It was handsomely bound with an illustrated and coloured cover and sold for the remarkable price of 6d. The part of Aladdin was played by Grace Leigh, the Princess Celestine by Evelyn Harrison, the Emperor of China by A. G. Spry and the villain, Hanki Panki the magician, by Joseph Wilson.

Every year of Mrs Nye Charts reign, she invited all the inmates and the whole staff of the Brighton Workhouse to a free performance of the pantomime. As there were about eleven hundred of them it seems likely that a special performance for them alone was given at the end of the run. After their visit in 1888 an illuminated address, dated 18th April and signed by eight officers of the Workhouse on behalf of all those who attended, was presented to Mrs Nye Chart and now hangs in the theatre. It spoke of the weeks of eager expectation with which the inmates looked forward to this only pleasure in their drab lives and the many weeks afterwards during which it was remembered and discussed. The inscription ended with this moving tribute: 'Many of us will, on the next reoccurrence of your invitation, be in the world of shadows, but when we meet at the last great transformation scene, the things which you have done for the poor and friendless will be written in letters of gold above your head.' It was such very unusual kindnesses as these invitations which accounted for Ellen Nye Chart's great popularity at the time of her early death.

By the early eighteen-eighties the theatre was very prosperous indeed. On 16th October 1883 Mrs Nye Chart bought the freehold of her own house, No. 9 New Road, for £1,800 with a mortgage of £1,600. A year later, on 5th December 1884, she paid off the sum of £6,000 advanced to her husband under mortgage by the syndicate which had helped him to buy the theatre in 1866. In January 1888 she paid off the £1,6000 mortgage on her home. In 1889 she was only 48 years old. But she must evidently have felt that it was time for the theatre to be placed on a more permanent footing than her own sole ownership and management. Therefore a limited liability company known as the Brighton Theatre Royal Limited was formed with an authorised capital of £30,000, consisting of 500 5% preference shares of £10 each, and 2,500 ordinary shares of £10 each. This was registered with the Registrar of Joint Stock Companies on 7th February 1889.

At the same time Mrs Nye Chart agreed to sell the theatre and her own house, No. 9 New Road, to the company for £43,000. Of this, £20,000 represented the price of the actual buildings of the theatre and No. 9 New Road. At the same time, acting under the powers conveyed on a tenant holding a long lease by the Conveyancing Acts, 1881 and 1882, she entered into a deed which declared that the 999 years leasehold of the theatre was enlarged into a fee simple or freehold.

The purchase price was paid, as to £23,00 in cash, as to £15,000 in the issue of her of 150 debentures of £100 each, and as to £5,000 in the issue to her or to her nominees of 500 preference shares of £10 each. Of this last amount, £200's worth of preference shares were in fact issued to nominees, namely £100 to George Clayton of No. 13 St Donat's Road, New Cross, who was described in the minutes of the company as Cattle Salesman, and £100 to Jean Ignace Verdié of St Helen's Lodge, West Brighton, who was described as Gentleman.

The first Directors of the company were Mrs Nye Chart herself, J. I. Verdié, who has already been mentioned as her nominee, Henry John Infield of No. 130A North Street, Brighton, who was Chairman of the Southern Publishing Company, and James Fraser of No. 169 Camden Road and later of Tregarthyn, Eton Avenue, London N.W., who was an accountant[1]. George Rae Thomson Fraser of Leighside, Tunbridge Wells, who was probably James Fraser's brother, acted as Secretary of the company for a provisional period of one month but was replaced by D'Arcy Peskett on 7th March at a salary of £150 a year.

The first meeting of the Board of Directors was held on 9th February 1889 at the office of the Southern Publishing Company, 130 North Street, Brighton. All board meetings and annual meetings of the shareholders were held at that address until 1950, when the Southern Publishing Company moved across the road to Argus House, No 50 North Street. The Board of the theatre thereafter held their meetings there until 1961, when the Board was reconstituted and the meetings were transferred to 23 New Road or to the theatre itself.

At the first meeting Henry John Infield was appointed Chairman of the Directors — a post which he retained until his death in 1921. He and Mrs Nye Chart were appointed Joint Managing Directors with full powers to carry on the theatre. At a subsequent meeting on 14th February 1890 their remuneration was fixed at £416 a year for Mrs Nye Chart and £208 a year for Henry John

[1] James Fraser remained a Director of the Company until his death in May, 1902.

Infield, plus a further remuneration of £100 for every £2 10s. 0d. per cent of dividend beyond £10 per cent which may be earned upon the Ordinary shares of the Company.

They were given the free use of the theatre box at dress circle level on the off prompt side or to the left of the stage, which has remained the Directors' box ever since. Under the terms of the original agreement between Mrs Nye Chart and the company she was entitled during her life to the free occupation of Royal House, No. 9 New Road, which had been her home for many years. After a years's working of the company the salaries of the other two Directors were fixed at 50 guineas a year.

The first meeting of the Directors also appointed as solicitor to the company the Chart family's old friend, John Kent Nye, who had frequently appeared on the stage of the Theatre Royal and was then practising at No. 9 North Street. His firm, later known as Nye and Treacher of No. 58 Ship Street and later still as Nye and Donne (now Donne, Mileham and Haddock) retained their connection with the Theatre Royal until Charles Whittaker retired from the position of Director when the Board was reconstituted in 1961. The first accountant to the company was George Fraser, who was prbably a brother of the Director, James Fraser. His firm, James Fraser and Sons of 2 Tokenhouse Buildings and later Langthorn House, Copthall Avenue, London E.C. acted as accountants and auditors to the company until 1961 and auditors only until 1964. At the fourth meeting of the Directors on 15th February the first shares in the company were issued. The agreed amount of 150 5% mortgage debentures of £100 each and 500 preference shares of £10 each were allotted to Mrs Nye Chart (or her nominees, George Clayton and Jean Ignace Verdié). Applications had been received for 2,300 ordinary shares, out of the 2,500 authorised by the memorandum and articles of association of the Company. Mrs Nye Chart took 300 of these in addition to her debenture and preference holdings. Henry John Infield took 500 shares, James Fraser 210, George Fraser 50, John Kent Nye 100, and William Hallett of 141 Marine Parade, Brighton, who had been Mayor of Brighton in 1855, 500 shares. In addition to these there were 10 other shareholders, whose names are not of any note, taking between them 10 and 100 shares each. All these original shareholders were placed on the free list for seats in the dress circle.

At the first ordinary general meeting of the shareholders on 27th April 1889 an interim dividend of 10s. 0d. per ordinary share was voted. At the second general meeting on 25th January 1890 thc profit shown on a full year's working was £3,528 2s. 0d. This permitted the payment of a dividend of 5% on the preference shares and of 10% on the ordinary shares. During the year a number of improvements were carried out to the theatre. At the recommendation of the municipal sanitary engineer the sanitary arrangements were overhauled. A new Italian fireproof mosaic floor was put down. The passages to the dressing rooms were widened and new bars were installed in the saloon (now the stalls bar), the pit (at the north-east corner), the gallery and on the stage. The theatre was unusual in having a licensed bar behind the scenes. This was known, in recent years at least, as 'the gulp'. It survived until 1967, when it had to be removed to make way for a large new scene dock.

The pattern of the next two years was similar to that of the company's first year of existence. Though £918 7s. 7d. was spent on the redecoration and improvements in 1890, the profits for the year were £3,937 7s. 4d. In 1891 these amounted to £4,003 18s. 2d. As a result the same dividends were paid in each of these years as in 1889.

During the year 1891 the Hippodrome Theatre in Middle Street was completed. The Directors of the Theatre Royal viewed this development with concern and, despite the established position of their own theatre, rather spitefully opposed the application for a dramatic licence on behalf of the Hippodrome—fortunately without success. On 6th January 1892 the first transfer of shares in the company occurred. At the next meeting nine days later Mrs Nye Chart herself acquired another 100 ordinary shares.

On the last night of the pantomime *Cinderella* in February 1891 Mrs Nye Chart in her speech from the stage told the audience that 'there was scarcely a London novelty then running which would not come to Brighton during the present year'. She was as good as her word. In addition to such staple fare as the English Opera Company, the Italian Opera Company and D'Oyly Carte Opera

Company there were visits from a new opera company called the Horace Lingard Opera Company in *Favette* by André Messager, a new opera by Edmund Audran called *La Cigalle* and a French musical play without words from Paris and the Prince of Wales Theatre, London, called *L'Enfant Prodigue*. Herbert Tree made three appearances: in October with Fred Terry and Julia Neilson in *The Dancing Girl* by Henry Arthur Jones and twice in the next two months in *Lord Anerley* by Mark Quinton and Henry Hamilton. George Alexander and Marion Terry brought a play called *Sunlight and Shadow* by R. C. Carton and John Hare *A Pair of Spectacles* by Sydney Grundy. Charles Wyndham and Mary Moore played in *The School for Scandal* as well as in Robertson's *David Garrick*. Lily Langtry appeared as Rosalind in *As You Like It*, as well as in two other plays. J. L. Toole presented no less than seven different plays. Finally there was a special matinée of *The Monutebanks* by W. S. Gilbert with music by Alfred Cellier.

The Mountebanks, which was played on 25th February 1892, was planned by Mrs Nye Chart but not actually shown during her lifetime. Her foresight in making the theatre over to a company was to be justified more quickly than she had perhaps herself anticipated. During the early part of 1891 she was taken ill. Her heart was found to be affected, and she was warned that she should take life more easily. At first she complied and, following a holiday at Henley-on-Thames during the summer, appeared to be fully rehabilitated. During the rehearsals of the pantomime *Goody Two Shoes* she seemed to be in better form than before her illness. But once the pantomime was launched she had a relapse and was not able to make her usual speech from the stage on the last night of the run. A rest of a few days induced her to think that all was well again and on 3rd February 1892 she set out for London on business. She was taken ill on the train and, on arrival, had to go to the Grosvenor Hotel, where she was well-known. A Kensington doctor and later Sir Andrew Clark were called in. But she gradually sank and died at the Grosvenor Hotel on 23rd February 1892, aged only 51.

Her body was brought back to Royal House, No. 9 New Road, Brighton, where it more or less lay in state and the whole of the theatrical company paid their respects. The funeral took place on

Plate 8.

Ellen Elizabeth Nye Chart in 1876.

(Reproduced by kind permission of Mr. D. P. Kindersley.)

Monday 29th February. There was no performance at the Theatre Royal that evening. The service was held at St. Peter's Church and the Brighton and Preston Cemetry, where she was buried in her husband's family grave. Her funeral was one of the grandest ever held in Brighton, either before or since. The names of those present filled more than half a column in *The Brighton Gazette*. Henry Irving, Ellen Terry, Amy Sedgwick, Wilson Barrett, J. L. Toole and Lionel Brough all sent wreaths. The floral tribute from the staff of the Theatre Royal itself took the form of a lyre in violets with a broken string. Some evidence of Ellen Nye Chart's popularity is provided by the fact that wreaths were also sent by the Brighton cabmen, the officers and men of the Brighton Volunteer Fire Brigade and by the staff of the Brighton railway station. Her son alone was not able to be present as he was then acting in the United States.

Mrs Nye Chart's will and one codicil were made only one day before she died. After some minor legacies to a maid and to her brothers and sisters she left everything to trustees (her son, her fellow Managing Director of the theatre, Henry John Infield, and her friend and solicitor, John Kent Nye) on trust for sale for the benefit of her son. Her estate was valued at £37,916 14s. 4d., which was only slightly less than had been paid to her by the Company for the theatre in 1889. Thus during the sixteen years that she owned and managed the theatre she converted the mortgage debt of £6,000, which had been left by her husband, into a profit of nearly seven times that amount. This in itself was no small tribute to her business capacity. But what was more remarkable still was that, while doing so, she retained a heart of gold, as is made clear by the tributes paid to her at her death.

Her overall achievement, however, was wider than this. Her husband had assumed management almost in the age of the strolling player, certainly at a time when managers constantly defaulted and before the theatre was fully respectable. His achievement was to give stability to the Brighton theatre and to make it a respected institution. Mrs Nye Chart was able to build on these foundations. Her management coincided with the period when acting became a respectable profession. For instance, Irving was offered a knighthood in 1883, though he did not actually accept one until twelve years later. Stock companies were replaced by touring companies as the main fare of the Brighton theatre. This was a great improvement on the occasional visit of star players. It accustomed the audience to a far higher standard of performance. It also made Mrs Nye Chart's name known throughout the country amongst other theatres. Her achievement was to make the Theatre Royal one of the best-known provincial theatres in England and to give it national, as well as local, status. Hers was certainly the most important name in the first hundred years of the Theatre Royal's history, and since then Baxter Somerville alone has played as significant a part.[1]

[1] A bust of Mrs. Nye Chart stands in the dress circle bar of the theatre and a miniature version in terra cotta in the Managing Directors' office.

CHAPTER V

HENRY JOHN INFIELD AND H. CECIL BERYLL, 1892—1908

WHEN THE Brighton Theatre Royal Company Limited was formed in 1889 the first resolution of the Board of Directors had appointed Henry John Infield not only Chairman of the Board but also Joint Managing Director with Mrs Nye Chart. At the first Directors' meeting following Mrs Nye Chart's death Henry John Infield was appointed sole Managing Director at the same salary as had previously been paid to him and Mrs Nye Chart together, namely £624 a year, with full powers to run the theatre. But as he was not himself a man of the theatre one presumes that much of the day-to-day management and the choice of the touring companies to be booked was perhaps left to the Manager of the theatre, Arthur Wheeler, who had been in charge of the box office under Mrs Nye Chart.

But if not a man of the theatre, Infield was an important person in his own right, that is in the newspaper world. He was born in 1845 and had started in Brighton the first half-penny morning daily newspaper in the United Kingdom. Five years later he converted this into a penny paper, *The Sussex Daily News*. In 1880 he started another half-penny paper, *The Evening Argus*, and in 1896 *The Morning Argus* at the same price. These newspapers were in due course converted into the Southern Publishing Company, of which Infield was Permanent Director. He had various other business interests as, in addition to the Theatre Royal, he was a Director of Hanningtons Limited, of the Grand Hotel, of the West Pier and of the Brighton, Hove and Preston United Omnibus Company. He was also a Brighton magistrate. His address as a Director of the theatre was generally given as No. 130a North Street, Brighton, adjoining the office of the Southern Publishing Company. But he actually lived at a house in its own grounds which he had built for himself near the south end of

Plate 9.
Henry John Infield.
(Reproduced by kind permission of Mrs. Vera Codd.)

Ditchling Road. This was called Sylvan Lodge, Upper Lewes Road. Towards the end of his life he moved to the Grand Hotel at Eastbourne and died there in 1921.

On 14th March 1893 Mrs Nye Chart's place on the Board of Directors was filled by James Bradford of Oaklands, Haywards Heath. He was a rich man who was a great benefactor of charities. He built and endowed almshouses at Haywards Heath that are called after him and others at Helpston in Northamptonshire. He also provided a site for a hospital at Haywards Heath. He was knighted in 1915, presumably for these and other benefactions as *Who's Who* of the time does not mention any other achievement or any office held by him. When the Theatre Royal itself was in financial difficulties he provided a helping hand. He remained a Director until 1921, when he resigned on the grounds of age.

In 1896 Jean Ignace Verdié, who had been Mrs Nye Chart's nominee as a shareholder, resigned from the Board of Directors on account of asthma. His place was taken by Mrs Nye Chart's son, Henry John Nye Chart II. After going to Trinity College, Cambridge, he had adopted the stage as a profession at the age of 22. He made his debut at the Fifth Avenue Theatre in New York with William and Madge Kendal's Company in *The Queen's Shilling* by G. W. Godfrey. He first acted at the Theatre Royal, Brighton, apart from his appearances as a baby in a basket and with his mother at the age of eight, on 20th July 1891 during his mother's lifetime. The play was *This World of Ours* by Seymour Hicks. His London debut was at the Globe Theatre on 4th July 1892 as Ned Fellowes in *Ned's Chum* by D. Christie Murray. In 1896 he was living at Hathaways, Green Hill, Harrow. He remained a Director of the Brighton theatre until 1912, when he was living at Westbury, Carlton Road, Putney. He was then obliged to resign on account of undertaking another prolonged foreign tour. He seems never to have had the theatrrical success in England of either his father or his mother, and most of his acting career was in fact spent in the United States, where he often acted the part of the typical Englishman. He married an American named Violet Lota Morice in Boston in 1982. After the war broke out in 1914 he returned to England and obtained a commission in the Royal Field Artillery. He never acted again after the war and retired to Torquay, where he lived at Thanet House, Chelston. He had another spell as a Director of the Theatre Royal from 1921 until his death in December 1933 or January 1934. He had three sons and two daughters. The two latter are still alive.

During the years immediately following Mrs Nye Chart's death the theatre was run by Henry John Infield on the same lines as during her life and with equal theatrical success. The original production of all four of Oscar Wilde's plays was brought to the theatre at this time for a flying matinée. The first of these, *Lady Windermere's Fan*, with George Alexander and Marion Terry as Mrs Erlynne, came to Brighton on 14th April 1892. The play had been so successful in London that a burlesque on it had been written by Charles Brookfield and approved by Wilde himself. This appeared in London in May and was brought to Brighton for a matinée on 11th June. Wilde's second play, *A Woman of No Importance*, in which Lewis Waller played the chief male part, had a matinée in Brighton on 16th November 1893. The other two plays were shown in 1895 within a week of each other. Lewis Waller again played the lead in *An Ideal Husband* on 7th March, together with Julia Neilson, Charles Hawtrey and Charles Brookfield. Both Hawtrey and Brookfield unfortunately disliked Wilde. Brookfield was never in the first rank as either actor or dramatist, and in his case it was no doubt the envious hatred of an inferior for a superior talent. He even went so far as to provide information which formed the basis of some of the charges against Wilde at his trial. *The Importance of Being Earnest* appeared in Brighton on 16th March 1895 with George Alexander, Allan Aynesworth and Irene Vanbrugh.

In December of that year and again with a fortnight's interval between them there were two flying matinées of the original production from the St James's Theatre of *The Second Mrs Tanqueray* by Arthur Pinero with George Alexander and Mrs Patrick Campbell. Other appearances of note at this period were Edward Terry in *The Magistrate* and *In Chancery*, both by Pinero, in July 1892; F. R. Benson in *The Taming of the Shrew*, *The Merry Wives of Windsor*, *The Merchant of Venice* and *The School for Scandal* in September 1892; Janet Achurch in *The Doll's House* and *Hedda Gabler* in October 1892; Edward Compton and his company in

She Stoops to Conquer, *The Rivals*, *The School For Scandal*, *David Garrick*, *The Heir at Law* by George Colman the younger and an adaptation of Henry James's *The American* in November 1893; and Ben Greet in *Diplomacy* by Victorien Sardou in March 1894. A freak production in the same month as the last of these was a flying matinée of an all woman cast in *As You Like It*. It is some comfort that, our own age having produced an all male cast in this play, even the Victorian age was not immune from a similar idiocy.

The first two years of the new management seem not to have proved quite so profitable financially as in the last three years of Mrs Nye Chart's life. In 1891 the profits had been just over £4,000. In 1892 these fell to £2,405 8s. 0d. This was attributed to an epidemic of influenza during the pantomime and to the death of the Queen's grandson, the Duke of Clarence, immediately afterwards which cast a gloom over the whole country. In the following year the profits were again only £2,435 16s. 4d., which this time was—less credibly—attributed to a long spell of fine weather throughout 1893. In both years, therefore, the dividend paid on the ordinary shares was only 5% instead of 10%. However, this did not prevent the salaries of the Directors (other than H. J. Infield) being increased at the shareholders' meeting on 26th February 1894 from 50 to 75 guineas.

The first important task before the new management was the modernisation of the theatre. During the last two decades of the nineteenth century municipal authorities throughout the country were becoming much stricter about fire precautions in theatres, the want of which in previous periods had been responsible for so many theatres going up in flames. In Brighton in particular the Borough Surveyor, Francis May, had for some time been pressing the Directors to install a fireproof curtain between the auditorium and the stage, to improve the entrances and exits of the theatre and, above all, to make a better stage door. As two out of these three requirements involved the provision of more space the Directors were obliged to seek architectural advice. C. J. Phipps, who had rebuilt the theatre of 1866–7 and was a theatrical expert, was still alive and practising. He did not die until 1897. But the Directors do not seem to have thought of consulting him. They turned instead to a local architect who was not a specialist in theatre design. This was C. E. Clayton of Clayton and Black, then practising at No. 152 North Street, Brighton, (now Clayton, Black and Daviel, of No. 10 Prince Albert Street). The contractor was V. P. Freeman.

To a certain extent events played into the hands of the Directors. Mrs Nye Chart had enjoyed the free use of No. 9 New Road during her life. Her death placed this property at the Directors' disposal. It was consequently incorporated in the theatre itself. The ground floor, which had been a covered passage to admit scenery to the scene-dock behind, became the box office and the main entrance to the theatre. This not only gave access to the stalls, but provided new and separate entrances to the dress circle and the upper circle. The old staircase to the north of the Colonnade Hotel remained but became only a subsidiary exit from the dress circle. The former main entrance was converted into a separate entrance to the pit at the back of the stalls with its own bar. On the first floor of No. 9 New Road what had been Mrs Nye Chart's drawing-room became a new dress circle bar. Above this had been two storeys of bedrooms, in the principal room of which Henry Nye Chart had no doubt died. These became the manager's office.

There had always been two separate staircases to the gallery north of the Colonnade Hotel. In order to enlarge these the architect extended the whole building further east above ground floor level. Phipps in 1866 had added what Porter's *History of the Theatres of Brighton* had called a conservatory. But this was only a projection in the centre of the first floor. An addition was now made for the whole width of the theatre at this point (Nos 11 and 12 New Road) on the first, second, and third floors levels. This gave room for two new staircases of ample proportions to the gallery with access on the northern of the two at second floor level to and from the upper circle as well.

At the same time Clayton rebuilt the colonnade along the ground floor, but unfortunately not in the Ionic order to match the columns of the existing colonnade to the south. Instead he substituted a rather debased form of Corinthian columns about two feet higher than the exisiting Ionic columns. But the original intention was to make a clear break between the new colonnade on Nos 11

Plate 10.
The elevation of 1894 and of today.
(Photograph by John W. R. Barrow.)

and 12 New Road and that already existing at Nos 9 and 10. The Directors or the architect subsequently thought that it would be a good thing to extend the new colonnade across the adjoining houses. At first the owner and licensee of the Colonnade Hotel, John Christie, was not willing to give permission for this to be carried across his property. But after a while he agreed in return for the payment of £50 compensation and £30 costs. When the balustrade came to be erected in front of what was presumably his sitting-room window he objected to its height, and this had to be reduced. As the result of this work the new Corinthian colonnade, of slightly greater height than the old one and with a stuccoed balustrade, was extended across the whole frontage from No. 9 to No. 12. Where this joins No. 7, which has an iron balcony and Ionic columns below, the effect is uneven and spoils the uniformity of the colonnade as a whole. But in 1894 and for at least fifty years afterwards it looked worse. According to the minutes of the Directors' meetings the new columns were composed of terracotta supplied by Doulton and Company. These were unpainted. Within the last thirty years, when matters of amenity in street frontages have come to be considered of importance, the terracotta has been painted to match the other columns further south.

The plans of the new extension were approved by the municipality on 5th April 1894. This authority was not what would be described today as planning permission for a new building but was required in connection with fire regulations for a building licensed as a theatre. The drawings can still be seen in the archives of the Planning Department.

C. E. Clayton's addition can never have been a building of much distinction or one of the more interesting Victorian designs in Brighton. But as first erected it was more attractive than the building is now since the roof-line was then of some interest. The elevation was flanked by octagonal turrets with copper roofs. Originally these were balanced in the centre of the composition by a tripartite dormer window surmounted by an elegant curved pediment with finials. These three roof features were then linked to each other by a low parapet. This arrangement has been spoiled by the glazing of the space between the turrets in 1921 in order to form a foyer for the gallery and by the replacement of the curved pediment with an ugly brick panel which is perhaps meant to simulate a rectangular pediment but hardly does so. The result is most unfortunate. At third floor level the original design included five round-headed arches leading to an open balcony behind. These too have since been glazed to form a bar for the gallery at intermediate level and replaced by round-headed windows with iron balconettes. At the present day these are the principal feature of the elevation. But they are too high up to make much effect.

The problems of a new stage door were somewhat difficult and could not be solved without acquiring some access to Bond Street. The Directors first attempted to buy Nos 33 and 34 there, but this came to nothing. In November 1894 they therefore purchased Nos 35–38 Bond Street from the Huntingdon School Charity for £4,522. These were and are really a single building of cottage type which dates from the late eighteenth or early nineteenth century and must have been one of the original buildings erected in Bond Street when this street was formed. No. 35 was immediately converted into a new stage door, which it remains to this day. Nos 36–38 were re-let as shops, and a rent of £1 a week was obtained for No. 38 in 1896. They were resold for £2,650 in the depression of 1934.

The acquisition of this extra building also enabled better arrangements to be made for the handling of scenery and properties. At the same time the dressing rooms in the cottage wing were replanned and improved. But during the process the two green rooms disappeared. Mrs Nye Chart's tiny office on the first floor was replaced by a slightly larger room which at first was called the Treasury but later came to be used as the Manager's office. Baxter Somerville in particular worked here at a later stage of the theatre's history. The fireproof curtain required by the licensing authority was inserted. Opportunity was also taken to replace gas lighting by electricity. This was a fairly early case of electric light being installed in a theatre as the very first example was the Savoy Theatre in London, which C. J. Phipps had built for Richard D'Oyly Carte in 1881. The fittings of the old gas jets in the Theatre Royal were still visible on the back of the walls of the stalls until quite recently. A 'sunburner' was also installed in 1894. This was presumably some patent form of heating.

In addition to all this constructional work the theatre was redecorated at the same time. The ceiling was painted in geometric design with medallions representing different countries. The friezes showed figures of the great dramatists of the past carrying flowers. A new back-drop for the stage representing Windsor Castle from the river was painted by Tom Pilbeam. New seats were provided for the stalls. New carpets were supplied by Hanningtons for the stalls and the dress circle. These improvements enabled the Directors to claim, in the notice which was sent to the shareholders on 27th March 1895, that the theatre had been placed 'in the first rank, so far as the comfort and convenience of both audience and artists are concerned, and also with regard to the facilities for the production of the most elaborate modern plays'.

Special measures had to be taken to finance all this constructional work. As a first step the trustees of Mrs Nye Chart's will, who were the owners of all the existing debenture shares in the Company, were approached and agreed on 13th November 1895 to accept a reduction in the rate of interest thereon from 5% to 4½%. The architect's original estimate for the work, including the acquisition of Nos 35–28 Bond Street, was £11,000.

In order to raise just over this amount the Directors decided to issue 130 second mortgage debentures of £100 each bearing interest at 5% and redeemable by the company at £105 each on 24th June 1904. These were offered to existing shareholders only. The new Director, James Bradford, whose address on that occasion but on that occasion only was given as Snowdon House, Buckingham Place, Brighton, took up 70 of these shares. Henry John Nye Chart II, who had recently returned to England from his tour in the United States, and whose address was then No. 30 Montagu Square, London, took 40 shares. The remaining 20 were subscribed in equal shares by George Clayton of Garlock Villa, St Donat's Road, New Cross, and Mrs Ellen Taylor of 40 Canon Place, Brighton.

But as is usually the case, the architect's estimate was exceeded by nearly £3,000. At the shareholders' meeting on 7th March 1896 it was suggested that the remaining liability to the builders should be discharged by further borrowing. So the Directors subsequently decided to issue 30 third mortgage debentures of £100 each bearing interest at 6% and redeemable on 24th June 1906.[1] Only 13 of these debentures were originally subscribed at the time. The biggest subscriber was Charles Henry Nye of Ditchling Villa, Keymer, who took 5 shares. He was presumably a brother of John Kent Nye, who had been such a great friend of the Nye Chart family. Two shares were taken by George Clayton of New Cross in addition to his previous holding of second debentures and one by Frederick Wakefield Price of 49 Guildford Street, Russell Square, London. Clayton and Black subsequently offered to take 3 such debentures in part payment of their bill of £692 5s. 9d. for the work done by them. These were issued to them, and the balance of their account paid.

This £1,600's worth of third debentures really met all the outstanding calls of the moment. Therefore at the shareholders' meeting on 13th July 1897 it was decided not to issue the remaining £1,400's worth of third debentures for the time being.

The redecoration of the theatre had cost just over £900 and the installation of electricity £650. While the work was being carried out the theatre was closed for four months. The Directors decided that some of the employees' wages must be paid during that period. These amounted to £614 8s. 6d. These sums could be reckoned as part of the year's running costs of the theatre, but they reduced the profit for the year 1894 to £1,378 14s. 0d., as compared with £2,435 16s. 4d. in 1893. The two years following reverted to normal, when the profits were £2,382 1s. 1d. and £2,677 16s. 0d. respectively. But in view of the capital borrowing that had been carried out during the period no dividend was paid on the ordinary shares during the years 1894, 1895 and 1896.

The theatre re-opened on 1st September 1894 with a performance of *Little Christopher Columbus* a burlesque opera by George Sims and Cecil Raleigh with music by Joan Cargill. The price of seats was the same as it had been in 1876, namely, 5s. 0d. for the stalls, 4s. 0d. for the dress circle, 3s. 0d. for the pit stalls, 2s. 6d. for the upper circle, 1s. 6d. for the pit, 1s. 0d. for the amphitheatre (which was the front of the gallery) and 6d. for the

[1] They were not redeemed until 1951.

gallery proper. The seats in the pit, amphitheatre and gallery were all unreserved, but 6d. extra could be paid for entrance to any of these at 'early doors', which was half an hour before the normal time of admission. Complaints were sometimes made in the *Brighton Herald* that on popular nights the queues for 'early doors' obstructed the pavement under the colonnade in front of the theatre. Each row of the seats in the pit formed a single bench with a back. On crowded nights a 'packer' was employed to cause those seated in each row to move up in order to make room for more people. The old idea of admission at half price halfway through the performance, which had been in force as late as 1887, no longer applied. This was because the performance each night no longer comprised several plays lasting in total four or five hours. One play, perhaps with an occasional curtain-raiser, sufficed. The performances were therefore able to begin later. Those in Brighton in 1894 began at 8 p.m. The two matinées on Thursdays and Saturdays began at 2 p.m. Even as early as 1887 the telephone had been installed in the theatre, though one wonders how the theatre could benefit from it as there were then very few private subscribers. This is shown by the fact that the theatre's telephone number was 18.

After the rebuilding of 1894 an elegant new cover was designed for the programme of each performance. This cost one old penny. It showed vignettes of the new elevation in New Road, the entrance hall, the auditorium and the dress circle bar or foyer. Inside the programme it was noted that 'Bonnets are not allowed at Evening Performances in the first three rows of either Stalls or Dress Circle or in the Private Boxes.' There was also a note that the last train for London left at 10.30 p.m. (or 11.30 p.m. on Thursdays).

Immediately on re-opening the Directors announced that 'in compliance with a very general demand on the part of the public and some of the companies visiting the Theatre'[1] they had decided to abolish booking fees. This reduced the Company's income by £250 a year.

In December 1894 the D'Oyly Carte Opera Company brought to Brighton one of the two Gilbert and Sullivan operas written

[1] Notice to share-holders of the 27th March, 1895.

Plate 11.
Cover of the Theatre programme in 1897.
(Reproduced by kind permission of Mr. Henry Smith.)

after the famous quarrel between Gilbert and Sullivan. This was *Utopia Limited* which had only just completed its original run of eight months—then considered almost a failure—at the Savoy Theatre. This opera has probably never been seen in Brighton since, though it was revived in London for the centenary celebrations of the Gilbert and Sullivan operas in 1975. With it the Company brought *The Vicar of Bray* by Sydney Grundy and Edward Solomon. March 1895 saw another of Gilbert's operettas but one which was written with F. Osmond, *His Excellency*. The chief part was played by Robert Courtneidge, father of Dame Cicely Courtneidge.

The outstanding event of that year was the appearances on 29th June for two performances of the great French actress, Sarah Bernhardt. Her plays were *Fedora* and *La Tosca*, both by Victorien Sardou. It was at a performance of *Tosca* that Bernhardt later injured her knee when jumping over the battlements of the Castle of San Angelo in the last act and the stage manager had omitted to provide a mattress for her to land on. When the doctor arrived to attend to her his hands were so dirty that she refused to let him touch her. Permanent injury resulted, and eventually she had her leg amputated as the only way of avoiding the continual pain that she suffered. Bernhardt was an exact contemporary of Adelina Patti. Though Patti often sang in Brighton, this was never in opera. So her performances were always at the Dome with its old oriental interior of 1863 and not in the Theatre Royal.

In 1893 Herbert Tree brought his famous production *Trilby*, adapted from George du Maurier's novel, for no less than three flying matinées. Johnston Forbes Robertson appeared in *For the Crown* by François Coppée in October. The most notable event of the year was a visit by the Duke and Duchess of York, later King George V and Queen Mary, on 10th April, when they were staying with Reuben Sassoon at No. 7 Queen's Gardens, Hove, for a conference of the National Union of Teachers. The play was *A White Lie* by Sydney Grundy with William and Madge Kendal.

1897 began with an operatic flourish as soon as the pantomime was over. At the end of February the Carl Rosa Company for the first time made a visit of a fortnight with no less than twelve operas:- *Hansel and Gretel*, *Tannhäuser*, *Masstersingers*, *Rienzi*,

Lohengrin, The Flying Dutchman, Carmen, Faust, Romeo and Juliet, I Pagliacci, Cavalleria Rusticana and *Don Giovanni*. After only a week's interval a whole week was devoted to Dr, later Sir William, Villiers Stanford's new Irish opera. *Shamus O'Brien*. A month later Tree brought three plays to the theatre: *Trilby* again; *The Dancing Girl* by Henry Arthur Jones and *A Bunch of Violets* by Sydney Grundy.

During this year (1897) the management of the theatre decided to revert to the practice that had been in operation in the pre-Nye Chart era to let the theatre for a period of years. An extraordinary general meeting of shareholders was held on 25th March to authorise this step. No explanation of the move is given in the minutes of the company, but it presumably stemmed from the fact that the Chairman and Managing Director, Henry John Infield, was not himself a man of the theatre and had presumably tired of being personally responsible for the organisation of the theatre's programme, as had been the case since 1892. As a result, his salary was reduced from £624 to 100 guineas in 1898 and to 30 guineas in 1899 and subsequent years. In 1899 the salaries of the other Directors were similarly reduced from 75 to 15 guineas a year.

The theatre was let from 25th March 1897 for a term of twenty-five years, determinable by the lessee at seven or fourteen years, for a rent of £2,850 a year 'subject to stringent conditions with regard to repairs'. The lessee was William Harcourt Sparrow, who was professionally known as H. Cecil Beryll. By a deed of covenant of even date with the lease the rent was guaranteed by Robert Halford JP, Edward Compton Mackenzie and John Hunt. Just over a year later (October 1898) the lease was assigned by Cecil Beryll to these three guarantors, but for a period of eleven years or so in all he continued to act as the Manager of the theatre.

His policy was generally to maintain the same arrangements as had been followed so successfully by Mrs Nye Chart and Henry John Infield during the last twenty years. But he was not able to produce as many flying matinées as they had done. These became occasional rather than a regular event almost every Thursday. The first of these sponsored by Cecil Beryll was on 29th April when Violet Vanbrugh and Arthur Bourchier appeared in *The Queen's*

Proctor by Herman Merivale. During the week of 26th August a performer more often seen at the Hippodrome came to the Theatre Royal. This was Little Tich in a show called *Lord Tom Noddy* written by George Dance with music by F. Osmond Carr.

During 1898 the Carl Rosa Opera Company actually made two visits, for a fortnight in March and for a week in October. The Duke and Duchess of Fife, (Princess Louise), who lived at No. 1 Lewes Crescent and No. 14 Chichester Terrace, attended their performance of *Carmen* on 1st March. In addition to their usual repertoire the Company performed *La Bohème* for the first time in Brighton, also *Mignon* and *A Poet's Dream,* both by Ambroise Thomas, and a lyrical drama by Arthur Sullivan called *The Martyr of Antioch.*

On 26th May there was a flying matinée of Arthur Pinero's new play *Trelawney of the Wells,* with Irene Vanbrugh, Arthur Bourchier and Lord Rosslyn, who acted under the name of James Erskine. A small part in the play was taken by an actor who was later himself to be a star, Gerald du Maurier. He was the son of George du Maurier, who had written *Trilby.* On 7th July Sarah Bernhardt made her second appearance in Brighton, this time in *La Dame aux Camelias.* This year for the first time for more than twenty-five years there was no pantomime at Christmas. Instead Henry Irving and Ellen Terry's Company from the Lyceum Theatre, London, played in the theatre from Christmas Eve for one week. Irving himself was ill and unable to appear, but Ellen Terry gave *The Merchant of Venice, Olivir* by W. G. Wills, *Madame Sans Gêne* by Victorien Sardou and *Nance Oldfield* by Charles Reade.

The first event of importance in 1899 was a three weeks' season in January by Wilson Barrett. In addition to *Hamlet,* he specialised in strong dramas written by himself or adapted from novels by Hall Caine and others often with a Christian theme, set in the Roman empire. This time he presented *The Sign of the Cross, The Silver King, Ben-My-Cree, Claudian* and *The Manxman,* all of this calibre. A month later the National Grand Opera Company produced ten operas in eight performances, amongst which, in addition to the normal favourites, were *Maritana* by William Wallace, *The Lily of Killarney* by Sir Julius Benedict and *The Prentice Pillar* by Reginald Sumerville. A special matinée on 30th March was given by Gatti and Frohmann's Vaudeville Company in *On and Off* adapted from the French of Alexandre Birson, in which the future film star, George Arliss, played a subsidiary role. On 4th May Mrs Patrick Campbell appeared in a special performance of *Magda* by Hermann Sudermann. When the Carl Rosa made their next visit in June they were able to give the first performance in Brighton and second in England of a Chinese opera *San Lin* by Victor Hollaender.

An unusual event occurred during the week of 7th June 1899. The theatre had to be closed because the scenery of the play *The Great Ruby*, by Cecil Raleigh and Henry Hamilton, which was to have been performed, was destroyed by fire in the special train that was bringing it to Brighton. The play itself was, however, seen at the Theatre Royal the following year during the week of 7th May. On 6th July Benoit-Constant Cocquelin with his less well known son, Jean Cocquelin and their company from the Porte Saint Martin theatre in Paris gave a special performance of *Tartuffe*. Again in the absence of a Christmas pantomime the year ended with a three weeks' season by George Alexander and Henry Irving's son, H. B. Irving, in five plays: *The Prisoner of Zenda* by Anthony Hope, *The Ambassador* by J. O. Hobbes, *In Days of Old* by Edward Rose, *The Man of Forty* by Walter Frith and *The Masqueraders* by Henry Arthur Jones.

1900 began with a flying matinée of a very controversial play, Pinero's *The Gay Lord Quex*. On its first performance in London the preceding year, with John Hare and Irene Vanbrugh, the play had been denounced by the Bishop of Wakefield without seeing it as 'the most immoral play which has ever disgraced the stage of this country'. When it was played in Brighton, with Gilbert Hare and Fanny Coleman, the *Brighton Herald* commented that it was 'quite inconceivable that, if the Bishop saw the play, he would adhere to his opinion'. During the Carl Rosa's annual visit in March their unusual contribution that year was *Satanella* by Michael Balfe. This was followed in April by *The Rose of Persia* By Sir Arthur Sullivan and Basil Hood, which was produced by the D'Oyly Carte Opera Company.

The summer brought two Shakespeare companies: Julia Neilson and Lilian Braithwaite as Rosalind and Celia respectively in *As You Like It*, and F. R. Benson in *The Taming of the Shrew*, *Twelfth Night* and *The Merchant of Venice*, together with *The Rivals* and *She Stoops to Conquer*. The play shown during the week of 15th October was described by the *Brighton Herald*, 'as a fascinating little Japanese tragedy'. This was *Madame Butterfly* by David Bellasco, then quite unknown as Puccini's opera was not written until four years later. Just before Christmas Irving and Ellen Terry made another appearance in their old favourites: *The Merchant of Venice*, *The Bells*, *The Lyons Mail*, *Nance Oldfield*, *Olivia*, plus *A Story of Waterloo* by Conan Doyle. This was Irving's last appearance on the stage in Brighton, but with J. L. Toole he attended a performance of Cecil Beryll's own Company in *The Golden Age* by Vincent Brawn on 22nd July 1902. He died three years later. The year 1900 ended with a fortnight's visit by Fred Terry and Julia Neilson in the first of their romantic plays with which they were to return to the Theatre Royal again and again for the next thirty years: *Sweet Nell of Old Drury* by Paul Kester.

The beginning of the new century was overshadowed by an event which seemed to the English people at the time like an eclipse of a natural phenomenon, namely, the death of the old Queen. During the week of 14th January Wilson Barrett had been playing at the theatre in *Man and His Makers*, written by himself and Louis Parker. The following week he was to have given *Quo Vadis?* also adapted by him from the novel by Henryk Sienkiewicz. One performance was, in fact, given on the Monday. The Queen died at 6.30 p.m. on Tuesday 22nd January. People had begun to assemble for the evening performance at 8 p.m., when the news of her death was announced from the stage. The *Brighton Herald* reported that they 'mournfully departed'. The theatre was closed for the whole of that week and the following week. It re-opened for a visiting pantomime. *Puss-in-Boots*.

In February the D'Oyly Carte Opera Company made their annual visit. The chief singers at that time in succession to George Grossmith and Rutland Barrington were C. H. Workman and Fred Billington. When it was the turn of the Carl Rosa their unusal operas were *The Lily of Killarney* for a second occasion, *Cinq Mars* by Gounod and *The Cricket on the Hearth* by Carl

Goldmark. The week before this (11th March) Johnston Forbes Robertson and Gertrude Elliott had brought *Hamlet*, *Shades of the Night* by Captain Marshall, *Carrots* by Alfred Sutro and *The Sacrament of Judas* by Louis Parker.

The principal event of the summer was a flying matinée on 27th June with Réjane in *Sappho* by Alphonse Daudet. The *Brighton Herald* in reviewing Ellen Terry's appearance in *Madame Sans Gêne* in 1898 said that Brighton theatre-goers had already had the opportunity of seeing Réjane in this play. Réjane's earlier visit to London had been in 1894. I have not been able to find any evidence that she came to Brighton on that occasion. The week of 12th August saw the production of a new opera by Arthur Sullivan and Basil Hood called *The Emerald Isle* with Isobel Jay in the principal part. The year ended with the appearance on 16th December of John Martin Harvey who became Irving's successor after Irving's death. He introduced for the first time two of the romantic historical plays which, like those played by the Terrys, were to be seen again and again at the Theatre Royal during the next thirty years. These were *The Only Way* adapted from Dickens's novel *A Tale of Two Cities*, and *A Cigarette Maker's Romance* from the novel by F. Marion Crawford.

It was such romantic plays as these and musical comedies or operettas which were to form the staple theatrical diet of the Edwardian period. Amongst musical comedies, for instance, there were in 1902 performances of *The Geisha*, *San Toy* and *My Lady Molly*, all by Sydney Jones, as well as of *Floradora* and *The Country Girl*. In the realm of romantic plays Charles Wyndham and Mary Moore brought their old favourite *David Garrick* by Tom Robertson and *Rosemary* by Louis Parker and Murray Carson. Lewis Waller appeared in *Monsieur Beaucaire* by Booth Tarkington at a flying matinée on 13th November.

There was also some more serious fare during the year. In April the Ben Greet Shakespeare Company made what seems to have been its first visit to the Theatre Royal, though Ben Greet himself had appeared there previously in plays not by Shakespeare. His Company had been formed as far back as 1886. So they had perhaps come to Brighton before as they occasionally played in the theatre on one of the piers. On this occasion the Company presented *Romeo and Juliet, The Merchant of Venice, Much Ado About Nothing* and *Twelfth Night*. On 19th June the students of the Guildhall School of Music presented a flying matinée of a new opera by Hermann Goetz called *The Taming of the Shrew*. On 10th July Sarah Bernhardt made her third visit to Brighton, again in *La Dame aux Camelias*.

1903 proved a year of considerable variety in the theatre. The Carl Rosa in April gave eight operas, including *André Chenier* by Umberto Giordano; the D'Oyly Carte Opera Company six works of Gilbert and Sullivan. There were two operas by Edmond Audran for a week each: *La Toledad* and *La Poupée*. *Merrie England*, which had first been produced in 1902, came twice, on the second occasion together with another musical comedy also by Edward German and Basil Hood, *The Princess of Kensington*. The romantic school was represented by Wilson Barrett and Lillah MaCarthy in four of Wilson Barrett's old plays and by Martin Harvey in a flying matinée on 28th May of *The Exile* by Lloyd Osbourne and Austin Strong. This play represented Napoleon at St Helena. Anyone less like Napoleon in looks, manner or character than Martin Harvey it is perhaps impossible to imagine! Ellen Terry, this time with Matheson Lang, made a week's visit on 23rd November in *Much Ado About Nothing;* the trial scene from *The Merchant of Venice; Nance Oldfield; Punchinello* adapted from the French by Hubert Carter and *The Mistress of the Robes* by Clothilde Graves. Charles Wyndham and Mabel Terry-Lewis appeared in *Mrs Gorringe's Necklace* by H. H. Davis and Cyril Maude and Ellis Jeffreys in *Cousin Kate* by the same author. Marie Tempest made her first appearance in a play which was to be one of the great successes of her career, *The Marriage of Kitty* by Cosmo Gordon Lennox. One act from it was even to be incorporated in her golden jubilee matinée in 1935.

The lease of the theatre to Cecil Beryll in 1897 provided that he or his assignees could break the tenancy after seven years. When the opportunity occurred the assignees informed the landlords that they would determine the lease on 24th March 1904. Cecil Beryll then made another offer to take the theatre on a new lease for seven years but otherwise on the same terms. This was authorised by an extraordinary general meeting of the company on 25th

November 1903, and a new lease was granted from 25th March 1904. The guarantors this time were Robert Halford and John Henry Sparrow, who was perhaps William Harcourt Sparrow, *i.e.* Cecil Beryll's, father.

Following this new lease the theatre was closed from 11th June to 24th July 1904 for redecoration. This was carried out by Clayton and Black of North Street at the cost of between £1,500 and £2,000. The ceiling was painted with designs of the four seasons; the frieze and the front of the dress circle with scenes from Shakespeare. A new back-drop for the stage was painted by Tom Pilbeam to represent Warwick Castle set in drapery of curtains with bouquets of flowers. The prevailing hue in the theatre decoration was said to be ruby.

The year 1904 did not produce as many memorable productions as was usual in the previous decade. F. R. Benson brought *Hamlet*, *The Taming of the Shrew* and *As You Like It* on 11th April. Fred Terry and Julia Neilson appeared in a, for them, unusual play, namely a wild western called *Sunday* by Thomas Raceward and on 21st September Ellen Terry again brought *Much Ado About Nothing*, *The Merchant of Venice* and *Nance Oldfield*, together with *The Good Hope* by H. Heijermans.

The pattern of 1905 was fairly similar. Martin Harvey came twice with a play that was to be another of his favourites, *The Breed of the Treshams* by John Rutherford, together with *The Only Way* on the first occasion. Fred Terry and Julia Neilson brought the second of their romantic plays *The Scarlet Pimpernel,* adapted from Baroness Orczy's novel. In addition to F. R. Benson with eight plays by Shakespeare there was a whole week of *The Tempest* with Iris Hoey as Ariel. Ellen Terry, this time with Hilda Trevelyan, brought a new play on the 18th September, *Alice-Sit-by-the-Fire* by J. M. Barrie. Marie Tempest, with Allan Aynesworth, appeared in another play by Cosmo Gordon-Lennox Called *The Freedom of Suzanne*. There was also a revival of *Lady Windermere's Fan* with the future film star C. Aubrey Smith, Ben Webster and Marion Terry. One more unusual event was the appearance of H. G. Pelissier's Company in *The Follies* — a revue which was to have a number of successors in later periods.

The Carl Rosa's selection in 1906 comprised, *inter alia, Fidelio* which had never before, or perhaps since, been played in Brighton, and *The Bohemian Girl* by Balfe. Mrs Patrick Campbell starred in *The Whirlwind* by Henri Bernstein during the week of 30th April. Two flying matinées of importance were given in May. One was of Martin Harvey in *Boy O'Carroll* by B. M. Dix and E. C. Sutherland on 31st and the other a week earlier of Ellen Terry in *Captain Brassbound's Conversion,* which Shaw had written specially for her as far back as 1899. This performance was notable for two different reasons; first because 1906 was the fiftieth anniversary of Ellen Terry's appearance on the stage and secondly because this was the first occasion a play by Bernard Shaw was played at the Theatre Royal. In November when Violet Vanbrugh and Arthur Bourchier brought, not for the first time, *The Walls of Jericho* by Alfred Sutro the *Brighton Herald* reported that Henry John Nye Chart II 'gave a telling rendering'[1] of the part of Dallas. He was to appear again there in May 1907 as Sir Marcus Ordeyne in *The Morals of Marcus* by William J. Locke.

Throughout the ten years from 1897 onwards the theatre was outwardly prosperous in that the Brighton Theatre Royal Company made a profit of approximately £2,900 each year and paid a divident of 5% on its ordinary shares. But things were not so well beneath the surface. Cecil Beryll evidently lacked Mrs Nye Chart's magic touch. Star actors were less frequently seen, and flying matinées became less numerous. The redecoration of the theatre in 1904, which was imposed by the terms of the lease, must have set the tenant back financially as £1,500 to £2,00 was a large sum of money at that date. At any rate Cecil Beryll was soon in financial difficulties. By August 1906 the rent of the theatre was in arrears, and application for this had to be made to the guarantors, Robert Halford and John Henry Sparrow. As a result the lease was assigned to them, as had happened with the earlier lease. Cecil Beryll, however, continued to manage the theatre for at least another year. On 8th June 1907 the *Brighton Herald* reported that he was giving up the management, having thrown in his lot with Emma and Percy Hitchison. The latter was the nephew of Charles Wyndham and after acting in his uncle's company, had gone into management on his own.

[1] 24th November, 1906.

Though the theatre continued to be run in much the same manner after the assignment the quality of productions in the first years of the new century was not quite what it had been in the last years of Queen Victoria's reign. Evidence of this can be seen in the flying matinées of 13th June 1907, which was the American play *Mrs Wiggs of the Cabbage Patch* by A. H. Rice and A. C. Flexner. There were, however, better plays. On 16th September Ellen Terry again brought *Captain Brassbound's Conversion*, this time for a whole week. On this occasion a part in the play was taken by her last husband, James Carew. During the Carl Rosa's annual visit they had intended to give Verdi's *Othello* but were prevented from so doing by the illness of their principal singer, Julius Walther. They gave instead *Rigoletto* and *inter alia*, *The Merry Wives of Windsor* by Otto Nicolai. John Hare made his farewell appearance in Brighton during the week of 2nd December in three of his old plays: *Caste*, *A Pair of Spectacles* and *The Gay Lord Quex*. In his speech from the stage on the last night he invited the audience to continue to support 'this beautiful and well-managed theatre'.[1]

In the week of 10th February 1908 H. B. Irving brought two of his father's old plays: *The Bells* and *The Lyons Mail*, as well as *Hamlet* and *King René's Daughter*, adapted from the French by Theodore Martin. During the whole of this week King Edward VII was staying for convalescence at his daughter the Princess Royal's house in Lewes Crescent and Chichester Terrace while she and her husband, the Duke of Fife, were in Gibraltar. But strangely enough, despite his love of the theatre, the King did not attend any of these performances. Perhaps he remembered Sir Henry Irving too well in the parts. As the result England's most theatrically-minded King never in fact attended the Theatre Royal, although it had been visited by his mother and his son, neither of whom had anything like his fascination for the stage.

6th May saw one of the few occasions when the Theatre Royal was outshone theatrically by another Brighton theatre, when Puccini's new opera *Madama Butterfly* had a flying matinée at the Hippodrome. On 4th June Sarah Bernhardt made her fourth appearance in Brighton. She again gave *La Dame aux Camelias*

[1] *Brighton Herald*, 7th December, 1907.

but, as she had already been seen twice before at the Theatre Royal in this play and 4th June proved to be a very hot day, the matinée was not well attended.

When at the end of 1907 John Hare had invited the audience to continue its support of the Brighton theatre he was speaking somewhat prophetically or may havc had more knowledge than was then public. In February 1908 Robert Halford and John Henry Sparrow reported to the landlord company that they were running the theatre at a loss and asked for a reduction of rent. An extraordinary general meeting of shareholders was held on 14th March to consider their request but declined to comply with it. As a result the lessees assigned their lease in October to William Ernest Bode and Edward Compton Mackenzie.

CHAPTER VI

ROBERT LAWSON LAMBERT, 1908—1936

IN 1908 the partnership of Compton and Bode already had an established reputation in the theatrical world. Edward Compton Mackenzie, who was known in the theatre as Edward Compton, was born in 1854. He was the son of Charles Mackenzie and Emmeline Montague. He first appeared on the stage in Bristol in 1873 and in London, at Drury Lane Theatre, in 1877. In 1881 he was living at No. 38 Kensington Gardens, Brighton, and on 12 June of that year married at St Peter's Church, Brighton, Virginia Frances Bateman of No. 81 Grand Parade, Brighton, daughter of Hezekiah Linthicam Bateman of New York, presumably also an actress. The next year Compton formed his own company, the Compton Comedy Company, with eventually a repertoire of fifty plays, and proceeded to manage several London and provincial theatres. He is probably best known today as the father of the author, Sir Compton Mackenzie, and of Fay Compton who was a leading acress in the nineteen-twenties and thirties. She played Aunt Anne Forsyte in the first instalment of the *Forsyte Saga* television programme and died at No. 10 Eaton Gardens, Hove, in 1978.

William Ernest Bode, who was known in the theatre as Milton Bode, was nine years younger than Edward Compton. His first production was at a public hall in Taunton in 1887. He then financed touring companies. When in partnership with Edward Compton they jointly managed theatres at Dalston, Leicester, Reading, Wolverhampton, Huddersfield, Northampton and Chester.

Compton and Bode naturally needed a manager for the new theatre in which they had acquired an interest and to this position they appointed a man who was subsequently to have a big theatrical reputation and to be the most important name in the history of the Brighton theatre between Mrs Nye Chart and Baxter Somerville. His name was Robert Lawson Lambert.

With Lawson Lambert we enter the realm of living memory as several people besides myself remember him. He was born in Bombay on 29th August 1870. His parents were Henry Wise Lambert and Beatrice, née Beadle. The father was, perhaps an Indian civil servant. The son was educated at Dover College. Like most theatrical managers of the period, his first connection with the stage was as an actor. He played with Willie Edouin and with Edward Terry, who was also a well-known theatre manager. Then he became the business manager at Terry's Theatre and at the Garrick Theatre in succession. In 1896 he was appointed Assistant Manager at the Brixton Theatre. He was promoted to be Manager in 1899 and remained there until 1903. Then followed a period of one year at the King's Theatre, Hammersmith, and four years (1904 to 1908) at the Grand Theatre, Croydon. At some time during this period, probably in 1893, he married Ella York. They had one daughter.

The first action of the new management at the Theatre Royal was, with the consent of the Directors, to reduce the price of the seats at all but star performances, except for the amphitheatre and gallery which remained at 1s. 0d. and 6d. respectively. The stalls became 4s. 0d. (instead of 5s. 0d.), the dress circle 3s. 0d. (instead of 4s. 0d.), the pit stalls 2s. 6d. (instead of 3s. 0d.), the upper circle 2s. 0d. (instead of 2s. 6d.) and the pit 1s. 0d. (instead of 1s. 6d.).

Milton Bode was a specialist in the production of pantomimes. Therefore the new management reverted immediately to the old practice of putting on a pantomime in Brighton for Christmas which ran for about six weeks. In 1908 this was *Red Riding Hood*.

George Edwardes's production of *The Merry Widow* reached Brighton on 12th April 1909. But this was two years after the original performance at Daly's Theatre in London. One feels that Mrs Nye Chart would have had this opera in Brighton during the first summer of its run. On 13th May Martin Harvey gave a performance of Dion Boucicault's old play, *The Corsican Brothers*, at a flying matinée.

Under the terms of the lease of 1904 a redecoration of the theatre was due in 1909. The lessees tried to have this waived, but the Directors of the theatre refused to agree to this. During the month's closure that was then normal for the theatre in June or July the theatre was therefore completely redecorated. The figure and decorative painting on the fronts of the circules was replaced by moulded embellishments of cupids and floral designs modelled in white on gold or in gold on a surface of delicately shaded colour. The fronts of the boxes were faced with bronze panelling. The ceiling was repainted in gold and white, lightly touched with green.

Soon after re-opening on 26th July Forbes-Robertson brought his favourite play *The Passing of the Third Floor Back* by Jerome K. Jerome. A month later when the D'Oyly Carte Opera Company made their annual visit. The parts previously played by C. H. Workman were taken for the first time by Henry Lytton, who was to continue playing them for about another twenty four years. The last quarter of the year brought the Carl Rosa in eight different operas, Frank Benson in eight plays by Shakespeare and Cavaliere F. Castellano's Italian Opera Company, also in eight operas, one of which was *Zaza* by Leoncavallo. The year ended with Milton Bodc's pantomimc *Cinderella.*

On 24th March 1910 there was an unusual flying matinée in the form of a Sicilian company who presented a play named *Omerta* or *The Law of Silence.* A week later there was a performance of the first play by Somerset Maugham to be shown in Brighton, *The Tenth Man.* When King Edward VII died on 6th May the play running was *Fires of Fate* by Conan Doyle, but the theatre seems not to have closed at all, except possibly the actual night of the King's death. When the Carl Rosa Company came in October their unusual operas were *The Queen of Sheba* by Goldmark and for its first performance in England, *Destiny (La Forza del Destino)* by Verdi. In November H. B. Irving played in *Dr. Jekyll and Mr Hyde.* The year ended with a visit from Thomas Beecham's Opera Comique Company in *Tales of Hoffmann* and *The Bat* and with Milton Bode's pantomime, *His Cat and Dick Whittington.*

The lease of the theatre was due to expire in 1911. The lessees therefore offered to renew this if the rent was reduced from £2,850 a year to £2,000 and the insurance coverage lowered to £21,000. The Directors of the theatre were not willing to go below £2,650.

So the tenancy collapsed on 25th March 1911. But Milton Bode agreed to produce a pantomime at Christmas in return for 60% of the takings. This Christmas arrangement was repeated until 1916.

With the lease would have also lapsed Lawson Lambert's position as manager. In fact the *Brighton Herald* had reported as far back as May 1910 that he was shortly leaving. He had already established such a reputation for himself that the paper called him a 'man of exceptional personal qualities' and 'of unfailing tact and gentlemanly good humour'.[1] So when in November the Directors advertised the theatre in the *Era* and the *Stage* as being to let he approached them to suggest that they should resume direct control of the theatre and appoint him their Manager. No replies to their advertisements which the Directors considered satisfactory were in fact received. So in January 1911 the Directors resolved to take this step and formally appointed Lambert as Manager of the theatre.

Lawson Lambert in due course lived to be a considerable personage in the theatre world, but his original terms of engagement in Brighton were very modest indeed. He was paid £3 a week 'for attending to the engagement of companies and other business connected with the Theatre, such sums to include his expenses'. This salary can only be assessed in proportion to other payments if one remembers that a stage-hand was paid 22s. 0d. a week at the same time. The sum paid to Lawson Lambert must in any case have been a temporary arrangement for a trial period as by January 1913 the minutes of the Directors make clear that he was receiving a salary of £6 guineas a week, plus a bonus. He then asked for a contract for two or three years at a fixed salary of £400 a year. This seems to have been agreed. In the settled pre-war world salaries were not subject to regular increases. But as soon as the first Great War broke out the modern world experienced its first dose of inflation. It is therefore surprising that it was not until December 1918 that Lawson Lambert's salary was reviewed. This was then increased to £500 a year for three years, with a war bonus of £100 for 1918. By 1921 the bonus had become £150 a year, and two years later the sum of £50, expenses was added for the year 1922, with the grudging note in the Directors' minutes that it

[1] 28th May, 1910.

would be impossible to continue such a bonus in future unless there was a 'very considerable improvement in the business for the current year'. But the Directors evidently thought better of this niggardliness without waiting for the current year's profit to be known as only two months later, in March 1923, they agreed to a new contract for three years at £600 a year, plus £50 for expenses and an additional bonus of £50 if the dividend paid on the ordinary shares of the Company went above 10%. This it never did. No mention is made of what arrangement took place when the contract ran out in 1926. But in January 1929 Lawson Lambert applied for a rise and was granted a salary of £800 a year, plus £100 expenses. This seems to have been the highest figure that he ever reached during the twenty-five years he was employed by the Company.

The consideration of these figures has, however, led us a long way from Lawson Lambert's appointment as Manager of the theatre in 1911. The first crisis with which he had to deal was a fire which actually occurred at the very end of the tenancy of Edward Compton and Milton Bode. During the week of 20th February 1911 the play running was *Nobody's Daughter* by George Paston. On Monday evening the performance concluded normally, and the theatre was closed at 11.10 p.m. A fire must have broken out in one of the dressing rooms soon afterwards and burned without hindrance for about two hours. The Superintendent of the Fire Brigade afterwards said that another quarter of an hour would probably have been fatal. Two alarms were given by telephone at 2.10 a.m. on Tuesday 22nd and two horse-drawn fire-engines were on the scene very soon afterwards. They succeeded in preventing the blaze spreading to the theatre itself, but the dressing rooms burned out and the roof collapsed. All the costumes of the current play were destroyed. Nevertheless, with that ingenuity which has always characterised show-business in emergencies, costumes from the original production at Wyndham's Theatre were borrowed and despatched from London the same day. A performance was given that same Tuesday night in Brighton.

The dressing rooms were no doubt swiftly rebuilt, though there is no record of this. Internally they were somewhat replanned. But in dressing room No. 1a on the ground floor is a simple chimney-

-piece of slightly Regency character which may possibly be a survival of the old Manager's cottage, reset here after the fire. From the roof of the inner courtyard adjoining one can also see something of the north elevation of the old building which gives some indication of what the cottage of 1807 looked like.

There were two Shakespearean productions during 1911: *A Midsummer Night's Dream* on the 3rd April and Frank Benson on 2nd October with five plays, plus *The Piper* by Josephine Preston, based on Browning's *The Pied Piper of Hamelin*. 28th August saw the first appearance of Sherlock Holmes on the Brighton stage in *The Speckled Band* by Conan Doyle. But the most spectacular production of the year must have been the visit on 30th October of Russian dancers from the Imperial Opera House in St Petersburg (the Maryinski Theatre) whom Diaghilev had introduced to London that season. The chief dancers were Vallya Lodowska and Andreas Pavley. During the same week there was a flying matinée of *Man and Superman* with Robert Loraine and Pauline Chase. This was a notable theatrical week in Brighton because on the same day as the flying matinée Sarah Bernhardt was to be seen at the Hippodrome in the last act only of *La Dame aux Camelias*, the whole of which play she had already given three times before at the Theatre Royal.

In 1912 the theatre was closed for the whole months of June and July for redecoration and rebuilding. A claim for dilapidations amounting to £2,561 was outstanding against the former tenants, Edward Compton and Milton Bode, and their guarantors, John Henry Sparrow and the executors of Robert Halford, who had recently died. This was probably settled for about £2,000. The money was used for the redecoration of the theatre, though it had been refurbished as recently as 1909. The walls and balconies were painted in white and gold. As a contrast to the crimson carpet the seats were re-upholstered in cream colour. Tip-up individual seats were substituted for continuous benches in the pit and individual seats were also inserted in the gallery and amphitheatre. The four little boxes at the back of the dress circle were removed and ordinary seats substituted. A new heating system was installed and a new fire-curtain erected as the old one had been made unsafe by having been painted.

As the result of the fire in 1911 a long argument took place with the Borough Surveyor on the subject of emergency exits from the dressing rooms in the cottage. For a time at least he declined to allow the three rooms on the first floor to be used. Clayton and Black therefore designed for the Directors a new block of nine dressing rooms behind the stage in what were virtually the back gardens of Nos 35–38 Bond Street. These were built during the same period of closure for the sum of £591. The cost of the whole work amounted to £2,522 10s. 0d.

In their notice to shareholders in February 1913 the Directors claimed that the renovations effected had 'brought the House thoroughly up-to-date and have been received with much favour by the public and by the visiting companies, who have expressed great satisfaction with the improved arrangements for their comfort'. At the same time the Directors expressed a caution about the future in view of what was to be the most dreaded form of competition that the theatre generally had ever had to meet: 'The multiplication of Picture Palaces and the increasing competition of Variety Theatres[1] and other places of amusement at low prices is a matter of some concern especially as each year it becomes more difficult to find, and costly to provide, first class theatrical attractions all the year round."

The profit on the running of the theatre in 1910 was only slightly below average for the past thirteen years. But in view of the improvements needed to the theatre, which were not actually carried out until 1912, no ordinary dividend was paid in 1911. In fact, during the next four years (except for 1913) the profits amounted to only about £2,000 a year, which was about £700 less than had been normal since 1897. As a result a dividend of only $2\frac{1}{2}$% on the ordinary shares was paid in 1912 and 1913, 3% in 1914, and no dividend in 1915, when the first year of the war affected the takings. It was not until 1916 that full prosperity was restored. The profits then rose to well over £3,000 for the year, and a dividend of 5% was resumed. In 1912 the fees paid to the Directors were increased to 100 guineas each, except for Henry John Nye Chart II who had been prevented by illness from attending

[1] There were four of these: the Hippodrome in Middle Street, The Court in New Road, the Grand in North Road and the Alhambra in Kings Road.

the Directors' meetings. In the previous year the Chairman and Managing Director had received only 50 guineas and the other Directors 15 guineas geach. The new rates of payment remained in force for some years.

The theatrical tastes of the immediate pre-war years were very light: mostly musical comedies, operettas and light comedies. In the year 1912 no less than eleven weeks were given to musical comedies: *The Chocolate Soldier* (twice), *The Quaker Girl* (twice), *Our Miss Gibbs*, *The Belle of Britanny* (by the Brighton and Hove Operatic Society), *The Waltz Dream*, *The Merry Widow*, *The Dollar Princess*, *The Count of Luxemburg* and *The Arcadians*. Heavier fare was provided by the Joseph O'Meara Company in *The Huguenots* by Meyerbeer, *Romeo and Juliet* by Gounod and three other operas. F.R. Benson brought six Shakespeare plays, including *Antony and Cleopatra*.

The principal comedies were *Fanny's First Play* by Bernard Shaw with Charles Macdona, *The Honeymoon* by Arnold Bennett with Marie Tempest and Graham Browne, and *Milestones* also by Bennett together with Edward Knoblauch, or Knoblock as he was to call himself after 1914. At that time Knoblock's connections were with Worthing, where he lived at Beach House, but from 1923 onwards for some years he lived at No. 20 Clifton Terrace, Brighton. Two great favourites of future years made first appearances. These were *Bunty Pulls the Strings* by Graham Moffat, and Gerald du Maurier in *Passers By* by C. Haddon Chambers in November.

The pattern of 1913 was fairly similar. Twelve weeks were again filled by operettas: *Princess Caprice*, *The Quaker Girl*, *The Count of Luxemburg*, *Gypsy Love*, *Sunshine Girl*, *The Cingalee*, *Les Cloches de Corneville*, *The Dancing Mistress*, *The Dollar Princess*, *Hullo Ragtine*, *Oh! Oh! Delphine*, and *The Merry Widow*. *Peter Pan* was played for the first time in Brighton in September with Marjorie Manners in the name part. During the Carl Rosa's visit their unusual opera was *The Jewels of the Madonna* by E. Wolf Ferrari. George Alexander appeared at three flying matinées, for the first time in fourteen years. The first of these was with Irene Vanbrugh in *Open Windows*, by A. E. W. Mason and the other occasions in *The Attack* by Henri Bernstein and George Egerton. There was no period of closure during the summer this year. Instead the London Repertory Company appeared at the theatre for a whole month in four different plays.

In February 1914 Edward Compton, who had previously leased the theatre with Milton Bode, brought his own Company in what was by then a very old-fashioned repertoire, namely three plays by Lord Lytton: *Richelieu*, *The Lady of Lyons* and *Money*, together with Robertson's *David Garrick*. March saw the first appearance in Brighton of *Where the Rainbow Ends* by Clifford Mills and John Ramsey. The incidental music for this play was composed by Roger Quilter, who was born at No. 4 Brunswick Square, Hove, in 1877, as a tablet on the house records. On the night that war was declared the play running was Lehar's *Gypsy Love*. In October Herbert Tree who, like Alexander, had not been seen in Brighton for about twenty years, made a reappearance in *Within the Law* by Bayard Veiller. Shaw's *Pygmalion* was first played in Brighton in November, and the year ended with an unusual play in the form of a dramatisation of *Anna Karenina*. During the interval Lydia Yavorska, who played Anna, made a patriotic speech from the stage about the was aims of the British and the Russians.

If the theatrical fare of the pre-was years was somewhat low-brow, that of the actual war years had almost no brow at all. Leading actors seemed not to have gone on tour. The principal stars of 1915 were Matheson Lang in *Mr Wu* by H. M. Vernon and Harold Owen and Lewis Waller in *The Three Musketeers*. But the cast of a play called *Searchlights* by Horace Annesley Vachell contained the name of a future star then largely unknown: Lynn Fontanne. The highlights of the year were really some of the regular visitors: the 'D'Oyly Carte Opera Company, the Carl Rosa in six operas including *Aïda* and Benson's Company in seven Shakespeare plays. His leading actress was Florence Glossop-Harris, the daughter of the impresario Sir Augustus Harris, and minor parts in the plays were taken by Basil Rathbone. At Christmas Milton Bode for the last time produced his usual pantomime, which was *Sinbad the Sailor*.

As the war proceeded even musical comedies seemed to be in short supply, possibly because of the shortage of young men for the chorus. But in March 1916 C. B. Cochran produced a review called *More*. Cochran was a Brighton man. He was born at No. 15 Prestonville Road in 1872, as a tablet on the house now records, and was educated at Brighton Grammar School, After Aubrey Beardsley he was perhaps the best-known alumnus of that school. At the end of the year (4th December) there was a flying matinée of that personification of war-time inanity, *The Bing Boys Are Here*. More serious fare was represented by the Harrison Frewin Opera Company with seven opera programmes, by Matheson Lang in *The Merchant of Venice* and by a flying matinée of *Hobson's Choice* by Harold Brighouse.

The chief feature of 1917 was that no less than five weeks were given to plays by James Barrie. These were *A Kiss for Cinderella* (twice, the first time with Hilda Trevelyan), *Peter Pan*, *The Little Minister* and *Alice-Sit-by-the-Fire*. The former Harrison Frewin Opera Company, which had been renamed the H. B. Phillips Opera Company, made a visit of two weeks, during which they performed inter alia *Martha* by Friedrich Flotow and *Two Little Wooden Shoes (Les Sabots)* by Egidio Romoaldo Duni. Unusually enough there were two controversial plays. The first of these was *Ghosts*, which was advertised as 'the play which was banned for twenty-three years'. The second was *Damaged Goods* by Eugene Brieux, whom Shaw considered to be the greatest French dramatist since Molière. In the cast of the latter was a then unknown actor who was soon to become a star of the silent screen: Ronald Colman. When C. Haddon Chambers's play *The Saving Grace* was shown in December the chief actors were Charles Hawtrey and Ellis Jeffreys, but a minor part was taken by a young man aged 18, whose name was Noël Coward. For the first time since 1907 there was no pantomime in this year. Instead the Christmas play was *The Maid of the Mountains* with words by Frederick Lonsdale and music by Harold Fraser Simson and J. W. Tate. This precedent of a musical comedy for Christmas was to be followed for several years to come.

1918 was an uneventful year theatrically. The H. B. Phillips Opera Company was again perhaps the most interesting visitor, and their most unusual opera was *The Daughter of the Regiment* by Donizetti. On armistice night the play running was *By Pigeon Post* by Austin Page, which was one of the few war plays to reach the

Brighton stage during the actual war period. Another such play of more distinction was *The Burgomaster of Stilemonde* by Maurice Maeterlinck which Martin Harvey brought to the theatre on 13th January 1919. This was perhaps the best play that ever figured in Martin Harvey's repertoire. But the armistice did not immediately disperse the prevailing mood of war-time frivolity as the next week the play was *The Bing Boys on Broadway*. In May of this year Henry Ainley made a first appearance in *Uncle Ned* by Douglas Murray. The Terrys added *Henry of Navarre* by William Devereux to their repertoire. Cyril Maude appeared in *Lord Richard in the Pantry* by Sydney Blow and Douglas Hoare and Herbert Lomas in *Abraham Lincoln* by John Drinkwater.

In March 1920 Ethel Irving appeared in *La Tosca* which had not been seen in Brighton since Sarah Bernhardt's visit in 1894. A fortnight later saw the production of the first of the comedies of A. A. Milne which were so typical of the nineteen-twenties: *Mr Pym Passes By*. The leading parts were played by Irene Vanbrugh, her husband Dion Boucicault, and Ben Webster, but in the cast was a then unknown young actor named Leslie Howard. During the Carl Rosa's visit the Company included an unusual opera instead of *Cavalleria Rusticana*. This was *Pro Patria (La Patrie)* by Emile Paladilhe. The year ended with *Chu Chin Chow* by Oscar Ashe and Frederick Norton.

The first Great War, unlike the war of 1939–1945, was generally a period of considerable prosperity in the theatre, despite the low standard of theatrical composition then current. The Theatre Royal was no exception, and immediately afterwards a great boom in business occurred. A dividend of 10% was paid on the ordinary shares of the company from 1918 onwards, and the profits for 1919 rose to the record sum of £7,300 3s. 4d. A special bonus of 300 guineas free of tax was voted to the Directors in 1919 'in recognition of their services during the War'. But the same gift was actually repeated every year until 1925.

This prosperity coincided with a new regime on the Board of Directors. On 24th July 1921 Henry John Infield died of a heart attack at Eastbourne, age 76. He had been Chairman of the company since its formation in 1889, Joint Managing Director with Mrs Nye Chart from 1889 to 1892 and sole Managing

Director since then. In 1904 and no doubt with a view to succeeding him, his nephew, John Henson Infield, then of Highcliffe Lodge and later of No. 7 Arundel Terrace, Brighton, was brought on to the Board. On the uncle's death the nephew did in fact succeed him as Chairman of both the Southern Publishing Company and of the Theatre Royal. He held both offices until his death in 1942. In 1921 Sir James Bradford also resigned from the Board on account of old age, and Henry John Nye Chart II returned for a further spell until his own death in 1934. The vacancy caused by the Chairman's death in 1921 was given to George Francis Donne of No. 58 Ship Street, Brighton, who had entered into partnership with John Kent Nye and in due course succeeded him as the senior partner of Nye and Donne. He remained a Director of the theatre until his death in 1944 and was Chairman of the company for the last two years of his life.

The first post-war improvement of the theatre that was necessary was the re-seating of the amphitheatre and gallery. This was due to complaints having been made about the discomfort of the existing seats. Plans were prepared by C. E. Clayton of Clayton and Black and were approved by the municipal authorities on 27th May 1920. At the same time a kind of foyer or ambulatory was provided at the back of the gallery. This was contrived by glazing in the space above the parapet and between the flanking turrets and the central feature of the 1894 building. This entirely spoils the roof-line of that building, though it was designed by the same architect. An enlarged bar for the gallery was inserted in the mezzanine space between the gallery and the upper circle by enclosing what had been an open ornamental arcade. Round-headed windows with iron balconettes replaced the arches. These are now the principal features in the elevation of the 1894 building but they are too high to make much impression. At the same time the building was repainted and re-upholstered in blue and gold. The total cost of the work was about £900. The theatre was closed from 19th June to 18th July while these improvements were made.

The prosperity of the period also enabled the Directors to embark on a policy of expansion. The first step was the purchase in 1920 for £2,950 of the properties immediately adjoining the theatre on the north, Nos 13, 14 and 15 New Road.[1] No 13 was then, as now, a sweet shop. No. 14 was immediately let for £80 a year to Lewis Colman Cohen, who twenty-eight years later became Chairman of the Brighton Theatre Royal Company. In 1920 he was described in the Brighton directory as an auctioneer and estate agent. As he was then 23 years old it is likely that this was his first business premises. When a leaner period in the theatre's history arrived these three properties in New Road were resold, Nos 14 and 15 in 1932 for £3,200 and No. 13 in 1933 for £1,400.

More significant, however, was the purchase of the Colonnade Hotel or No. 10 New Road, which forms an island within the area of the theatre. This building was to prove almost a symbol of the fortunes of the theatre. In 1923, when the profits of the theatre for the preceding year had been £6,048 9s. 7d., the Directors were able to buy it for £7,000 and let the building for £500 a year. In 1935, when there was a slump in the theatre and there was actually a loss of £98 4s. 8d. on the preceding year's running the Colonnade Hotel was resold for £5,750 in order to reduce the bank overdraft. In 1953, when prosperity had again been restored and the profit for the preceding year was £2,416 2s. 6d., it was bought back for £5,900. The third acquisition of the nineteen-twenties was the purchase in 1927 of Nos 33 and 34 Bond Street for £1,750. These immediately adjoined the stage door on the north. Like the other properties, these were resold for £2,320 during the depression of 1934.

During the first decade after the war the shows performed at the theatre perhaps displayed as light improvement in quality over those of the previous twenty years, but they were far from being serious in character. The prevailing note was that of drawing room comedy. There were certain companies which made regular visits, usually at yearly intervals. The most distinguished of these were the Frank Benson's Shakespeare Company, which brought at least five different plays each time, and the Carl Rosa Opera Company which, in a fortnight, would put on eight or more operas. Amongst those given were *Mignon* in August 1921, *Samson and Delilah* by Saint-Saëns in May 1923 and *Don Pasquale* by

[1] The land on which they were built was conveyed by the Prince of Wales to Hewitt Cobb in 1807 at the same time as the theatre land.

Donizetti in September 1927. The D'Oyly Carte Opera Company came for a fortnight every summer, usually at the end of July during the Sussex fortnight of Goodwood, Lewes and Brighton races. Then there were the champions of the romantic school: Fred Terry and Julia Neilson and John Martin Harvey. In 1926 the Terrys chose Brighton for the première of a new play by William Devereux, who had written *Henry of Navarre* for them. This was *The Wooing of Katherine Parr*, which provided Fred Terry with a part more suited to his age and figure at that time than did the more dashing roles of Charles II, Sir Percy Blakeney and Henry of Navarre. In 1927 Martin Harvey also introduced a new play into his repertoire at Brighton. This was *Scaramouche* by Baroness Orczy.

Of individual performances, one fairly typical of the period was that of Owen Nares in December 1921 in the appropriately named play *The Charm School* by A. D. Miller and Robert Milton. A fortnight later Eugene Goossens conducted *The Beggars' Opera*. 1922 saw the first of the farces which were to run in succession for so long at the Aldwych Theatre in London. This was *Tons of Money* by Will Evans and Valentine with Yvonne Arnaud, Ralph Lynn, Tom Walls and Robertson Hare. The next week an early note of the future was sounded by the appearance of the Birmingham Repertory Company in four different plays. In July there was a week of Grand Guignol plays from Little Theatre in London.

The highlights of 1923 were the appearances of Henry Ainley in *Cromwell* by John Drinkwater in February and of Sybil Thorndike during June in *Advertising April* by Herbert Farjeon and Horace Hosnell, followed by the trial scene from *Henry VIII*. On the second night of the run she played in *Medea* instead.

The first production of mark in 1924 was *The Rat* by David Lestrange with Ivor Novello in the chief part. In September Matheson Lang made an unusual appearance as Mussolini in a play called *The Hour and the Man* by Frank Stayton. Later that month there was a performance of *The Way of the World* which, curiously enough, seems to have been the first time that a Restoration comedy was ever played at the Theatre Royal.

1925 gave Brighton audiences their first opportunity to see Shaw's *Saint Joan*, but not with Sybil Thorndike as the Maid.

Dorothy Holmes-Gore took her part, and the play actually made two visits during the year. In April Kate Cutler appeared in Noël Coward's *The Vortex*, which had made a sensation in London the year before, and in October Eva Moore, who was herself a Brightonian, played the lead in his newer play, *Hay Fever*. During the summer the review which was a successor to Pelissier's *Follies*, namely *The Co-optimists*, made a visit with their original cast of Davy Burnaby, Gilbert Childs, Stanley Holloway and Anita Elsom. The Christmas show was *No! No! Nanette*, which was a typical example of the musical comedies of the nineteen-twenties.

At the end of March 1926 there was a dramatised version of *Tess of the D'Urbervilles*. Following it the Macdona Players gave a fortnight's season of plays by Bernard Shaw. These were *Man and Superman*, *Pygmalion*, *Fanny's First Play*, *Arms and the Man*, *You Never Can Tell*, *Mrs Warren's Profession*, *The Doctor's Dilemma* and *Candida*. The principal actor to make an appearance that year was Cedric Hardwicke. He had made his name as Churdles Ash in Eden Philpotts's comedy, *The Farmer's Wife* but was not in the cast when this play had visited Brighton. On this occasion he was playing in another comedy by Philpotts called *Devonshire Cream*.

The continued prosperity of the theatre caused the Directors to think of enlarging its seating capacity. As far back as April 1920, though C. E. Clayton was still the company's architect[1], John Henson Infield had taken another architect round the theatre informally to ask his advice as to whether it was possible to insert additional seats. This was a very young architect named Joseph Emberton who was then practising in London but later became a Brighton resident. He was one of the pioneers of the modern movement in architecture, and one of his works, the premises of Peter Jones in Sloane Street, London, has since been selected by the Department of the Environment as one of the very few outstanding buildings of that style and period to be listed as of special architectual or historic interest. He was however not a theatre specialist and on this occasion advised that, though the back walls of the dress circle and the upper circle could be removed, no advantage would be gained unless the staircases and exits which the municipality had required to be built in 1894 were removed.

[1] He died in November 1923.

In 1925 he was consulted again and this time advised that more rows could be added to the pit, the dress circle and the upper circle but only at the expense of abolishing their bars. On neither occasion therefore did his visit give rise to any subsequent action.

The Directors did not take these unofficial consultations with Joseph Emberton as a final decision. In November 1926 they consulted as different an architect as it was possible to imagine. This was another man in London practice but elderly, a traditionalist and a theatrical specialist. His name was Sprague, After C. J. Phipps's death in 1897 Phipps's virtual monopoly of English theatre design was shared between Frank Matcham, W. R. C. Sprague, Thomas Verity and Frank Verity. In London Sprague had been responsible for the following theatres: the Olympic, with Bertie Crewe, (1890); the Coronet (1898); Wyndam's (1899); the Camden (1901); The King's, Hammersmith (1902); the New (1903); The Aldwych (1905); the Strand (1905); and the Ambassadors (1913). It is possible that W. R. C. Sprague himself was not still alive and practising in 1926. In that case the advice given must have come from his son. The minutes of the Directors' meetings only say 'Mr Sprague, the well-know theatrical architect'. The plans, when submitted to Brighton Council, were signed 'Sprague and Barton'. Whichever it was, he advised that the extension of the seating capacity was perfectly possible, would cost about £8,000 and would take eight weeks to carry out. When completed it would add about £30 per performance to the potential takings of the theatre, in addition to providing standing room for a large number of people at the back of the dress circle and the upper circle. The Directors therefore decided to entrust this work to Sprague. The plans were approved by the Town Council on 30th December 1926.

As usual the architect's estimate proved to be an understatement. The work took twelve weeks and cost £13,000. The theatre was closed from 23rd April to 18th July 1927, during which time the staff who could not be employed were paid half salary. The work was financed by means of an overdraft at the bank and by the issue of the remaining £1,400's worth of third debentures, which had been authorised by a shareholders' meeting as long ago as 1896. These were subscribed at 97% of their value by Sir James Bradford, who had been a Director of the theatre from 1893 to 1921 and had taken up 70 second debentures in 1894.

The work involved was wholly internal. The auditorium of the theatre, as C. J. Phipps had left it in 1866, was a complete horseshoe in shape. Sprague altered this slightly by giving the sides in front of the boxes a slight indentation so that the new shape of the house in plan became like the Greek letter Ψ. In doing this he removed one column on each side in the dress circle and the upper circle, but not those in the centre of these circles or elsewhere. But the main work was to remove the back and side walls of both these circles so that a whole extra row of seats could be inserted at the back in what had been a corridor or ambulatory, and two or three seats added on each side of four existing rows. In this process the pairs of small boxes at the back of the main dress circle boxes were converted into single boxes.

At the same time the whole auditorium was redecorated. The slightly florid Edwardian details of 1909 were replaced by simple mouldings in the more austere manner then fashionable. The circles and boxes were given new fronts. Wreaths and paterae replaced the cupids and floral designs. A wide frieze of arabesques was placed over the proscenium arch. In the ceiling the central chandelier was reset in three wide encircling panels separated from each other by mouldings interspersed with flowers and containing more paterae or garlands. The upholstery of blue and gold was replaced by rose du Barry and silver.

This redecoration brings the theatre to its present condition. Since 1927 the only structural alterations have been behind the scenes. Thus the auditorium as we see it today dates basically from the Phipps 1866 period and the decoration, except for the giant pilasters flanking the stage boxes and the central chandelier, from the Sprague 1927 period.

The theatre re-opened on 18th July 1927 with a performance of another comedy by Eden and, this time, Adelaide Philpotts: *Yellowsands*. This was somthing of a gala occasion as the Mayor and Mayoress of Brighton and most of the town officials were present. The Directors' minutes state that the public and the visiting companies expressed great approval of the alterations

Plate 12.
Photograph of the auditorium today.
(Reproduced by kind permission of the Directors of Brighton Theatre Royal Limited.)

which had been carried out. Three months later the management refused a visit by Gladys Cooper, who was then in her own management, as she asked for 70% of the takings of the theatre, which was considered too high. However she made frequent appearances at the Theatre Royal at a later date.

1928 was something of a reversion to the Edwardian mode as musical comedies abounded. In addition to the pantomime, *Cinderella*, the following shows with music were performed; *Sunny, Peggy Anne, Hit the Deck* (twice), *Lady Mary, The Girl Friend, So Long! Letty* and *The Desert Song* (at Christmas). In contrast the Carl Rosa performed *The Valkyrie* amongst other operas in September and Matheson Lang played in *Such Men Are Dangerous* by Ashley Dukes.

Two unusual visitors made their appearance in 1929. The first was Gracie Fields in *The Show's the Thing*, a revue by Archie Pitt, in January and the second George Robey in another revue called *In Other Words* in October. The great war play *Journey's End* by R. C. Sheriff was acted during three separate weeks that year. Sybil Thorndike and Lewis Casson were seen in a new version of *Madame Sans Gêne* called *Madame Plays Nap* by Brenda Girvin and Monica Cousens.

The following year placed an accent on Bernard Shaw as, in May, the Birmingham Repertory Company brought his then newest play, *The Apple Cart*, with Julian d'Albie as King Magnus, and a fortnight later the Macdona Players presented five other plays by him. In June Ivor Novello acted in his own play *Symphony in Two Flats*. The Carl Rosa's most unusual contribution that year was Puccini's *Gianni Schicchi* which they played twice, once with *Pagliacci* and once with *Cavalleria Rusticana*. At this period Fred Terry and Julia Neilson made a series of last appearances in their old romantic plays: *The Scarlet Pimpernel* in December 1928, *Sweet Nell of Old Drury* in December 1929 and *Henry of Navarre* in December 1930.

This post-war period was the heyday of Lawson Lambert as the Manager of the theatre. He had by then become a leading figure in the theatrical world. In July 1927 he was elected to the Board of the Theatrical Managers Association and, in order to qualify for membership, was allowed to acquire 20 ordinary shares in the

Brighton Theatre Royal Limited. He was also a Director of a company called Biofix Moving Pictures Limited of Black Lion Street, Brighton. This undertaking took photographs of visitors to the town and bound them in two albums which would then be flipped through to provide the illusion of a moving picture.

In appearance Lawson Lambert was most impressive. In the day-time he always wore a large bow-tie, and his evening dress tie took the form of a wide band like a stock, wound once round the neck and tied in a large bow in the manner of a traditional artist's tie. He looked in fact like an actor of the old school, already dressed to go on the stage in the part of a nobleman or a butler in an aristocratic household. To the staff of the theatre he was known as Father. George Pennifold, who is perhaps the last surviving member of his staff, remembers him as a strict disciplinarian but very just and a thorough gentleman. He lived first near the theatre, at No. 140a North Street, and later, in the thirties, at No. 11a Palmeira Mansions, Church Road, Hove.

The same period was also one of great prosperity for Brighton Theatre Royal Limited. For fourteen years in succession, from 1918 to 1931, a dividend of 10% was paid on the ordinary shares in the Company. But the alterations of 1927, which were aimed at accommodating a large audience and thus at making even bigger profits, were hardly completed before cold winds began to blow throughout the theatre world all over England.

As far back as 1913 the dreaded competition of 'picture palaces' had been mentioned in the Directors' minutes. The decade from 1925 to 1935 was the period of the great cinema boom. All the large super-cinemas in London date from these years. Some of these are now very interesting period pieces, and a few have even been listed as buildings of special architectural interest. In Brighton the first and much the best of the large new cinemas was the Regent in Queen's Road and North Street. This was designed by Robert Atkinson and opened in 1924. It was in its time a famous building, and architects from all over Europe came specially to Brighton to see it. Ironically, it is the only such cinema in Brighton to have been demolished. The much less interesting Savoy (now the ABC), the Astoria and the Odeon followed in the thirties and are still there.

Plate 13.
Lawson Lambert in 1936.
(Reproduced by kind permission of Mrs. Winifred Keates.)

But the cinema alone was not the only hazard of the times. The theatre, like everything else, was affected by the great depression that assailed the whole country, in fact western civilisation in general. In 1931 the minutes spoke of the 'falling-off of theatrical business all over the country' and of the increasing difficulty that was being experienced in booking suitable productions 'owing to the very large number of failures of new London productions'. Those companies that were willing to come often demanded minimum financial guarantees. In addition the Brighton theatre had to face the special competition of the Hippodrome, which had started putting on musical as well as variety shows and even straight plays. Owing to the larger size of its auditorium it was naturally a greater attraction to visiting and particularly musical companies. A further cause of the decline in business was less credibly attributed to 'cheap daily transport facilites by rail and bus to London'. The profits on the year's running in 1931 fell by over £2,000 and the dividend declared on the ordinary shares of the Company was only 2½%, instead of the 10% that had been normal for the past fourteen years.

The Directors decided to contemplate letting the theatre, as they had done before, from 1897 to 1910, if they could find a satisfactory tenant. This they were not successful in doing, though several approaches were made. So the old policy of booking touring companies continued. In January 1932 the great American actress, Ruth Draper made her first visit to the theatre for a whole week. Two years later she also gave a flying matinée on 12th June 1934. October 1932 saw the first performance at the theatre of a play by J. B. Priestley. This was *Dangerous Corner.* A week later Donald Wolfit appeared in Shaw's *Too True To Be Good*, and soon after this a Company led by Kate Cutler performed four plays by Noël Coward: *The Vortex, Hay Fever, The Queen Was in the Parlour* and *Home Chat.*

1933 saw two farewell appearances. The first was of the Carl Rosa Opera Company which gave *Madame Butterfly*, *Pagliacci* and *Cavalleria Rusticana*, *Carmen*, *Il Trovatore* and *Don Juan* — the Carl Rosa always anglicised everything. The Company did not go out of existence until well after the second World War and continued to make visits to Brighton. But on subsequent occasions they went instead to the Hippodrome and later to the newly opened Essoldo Theatre in North Street. It would be difficult to exaggerate the debt which the provinces owe to the Carl Rosa for their activities over more than sixty years. The standard of singing in the company in the nineteen-thirties was not high, though it became so after the war. But it was a remarkable accomplishment that they were able at all to take sometimes eight operas in one week or more in a fortnight to one town, When one thinks of what would be the cost today of such touring one wonders how they were ever able to do it. In the present period when a whole year in Brighton can pass without the visit of a simple opera company, except possibly for the Brighton Festival, the town is much the poorer for the disappearance of the Carl Rosa Opera Company.

The second farewell of 1933 was a personal one. When the D'Oyly Carte Opera Company made their annual visit in August Sir Henry Lytton appeared for the last time in the leading roles that he had been playing since 1909. Early in the following year Nancy Price appeared in *Nurse Cavell* by C. E. Beechofer Roberts and C. S. Forrester.

Meanwhile the financial position of the Theatre Royal continued to deterioriate. In 1932 the tenant of the Colonnade Hotel defaulted on the rent, and a new tenant had to be found at a reduced rent of £450 a year, instead of £500. The profit on the year's running in 1932 fell by another £1,000 to £846 16s. 4d. Though 2½% was still paid on the ordinary shares, the Directors agreed to waive their fees for the year. Other measures of retrenchment had also to be made. The bank overdraft was at first increased, and in 1933 the theatre's account was even moved from the Westminster to the Midland Bank, possibly to secure more favourable treatment. But as the depression throughout the country became more difficult the bank began to clamour for a reduction of the overdraft and, in order to secure this, Nos 14 and 15 New Road were sold in 1932[1], No. 13 New Road in 1933, Nos 33, 34 and 36–38 Bond Street in 1934 and the Colonnade Hotel in 1935. In 1933 in the hope of attracting more patrons the prices of the theatre seats were reduced, but there is no record of the

[1] No. 14 was repurchased for £6,000 in 1970.

amounts involved. At the same time the Directors were successful in securing a reduction in the rating assessment on the theatre from £1,434 to £904. In the years 1933, 1934 and 1935, for the first time in the history of the theatre since the days before Henry John Nye Chart, there was an actual loss of £498 16s. 1d., £98 4s. 9d. and £393 14s. 9d. respectively on the running of the theatre, and no dividend of any kind was paid on the ordinary shares. In fact, save for 1¼% in 1939, no further dividend was paid on these shares until 1951. Nor did the Directors again receive any fees until that year.

By 1934 no reliable tenant had been found. The theatre was closed from 26th May to 23rd July. The financial position was evidently so serious at this time that the Directors must have contemplated closing the theatre altogether. This we must assume from the fact that in August they gave Lawson Lambert three months' provisional notice 'as being fairer to him and avoiding possible liability on the Company if circumstances arose which would necessitate the termination of his engagement'. However, he did not leave at the end of that period as the prospects improved slightly during the second half of the year. The ever-popular D'Oyly Carte Opera Company, with Martyn Green in the place of Sir Henry Lytton, played to capacity houses in August. This was actually the company's last visit to the Theatre Royal until 1971. During the intervening years they did not cease to visit Brighton but went instead to the Hippodrome until that theatre closed in 1964.

At the end of November 1934 John Martin Harvey brought for the last time some of his old plays such as *The Bells*, which he had inherited from Irving, and *David Garrick*, which had been one of Charles Wyndham's principal plays, as well as *The King's Messenger* and a new contemporary play by Roy Jordan called *Beyond*. Although this was announced as a farewell visit, Martin Harvey did in fact act in Brighton on two more occasions. The next of these was in August 1935, when he presented a new play *The Scapegoat*, which was based on Dickens's novel *Great Expectations*. The last occasion was in April 1939. During the week of Martin Harvey's 1934 visit, a special matinée was held on 27th November in aid of the Heritage Craft School at Chailey, which

Princess Alice' Countess of Athlone, who then lived at Brantridge Park, Balcome in Sussex, attended for a fee of 40 guineas.

The next week Philip Ben Greet brought his Shakespeare Company to Brighton for the last time. They performed *The Merchant of Venice, As You Like It, Twelfth Night, The Tempest, Macbeth* and *The School for Scandal.* As in the case of the Carl Rosa Opera Company, the provincial theatre owes an incomparable debt to this Company and that of Frank Benson for having almost every year for over forty years brought five or six different Shakespeare plays to each theatre where they made a week's stand. About seven years later Donald Wolfit's Company took their place and operated for another decade. But since that time Brighton is lucky if it sees a single Shakespeare play for a whole week even once a year. This is a sad falling-off. The year 1934 ended with a visit from the Anton Dolin Ballet Company.

While these events were taking place the Directors were considering the possibility of a repertory season in 1935. On 14th November 1934 there appears for the first time in the Directors' minutes the name of the man who was to succeed Lawson Lambert in the running of the theatre and was to be the most important person in its history since Ellen Nye Chart, namely John Baxter Somerville. His story belongs to the next chapter, but he was then running the Croydon Repertory Theatre. Lawson Lambert had been Manager of the Grand Theatre at Croydon as far back as 1904 to 1908. In the desperate search for visiting companies to play at Brighton he had introduced the Croydon Repertory Company to the Theatre Royal on two occasions in 1934. During the week of 30th April they had played in *Sheppey* by Somerset Maugham and during the week of 6th June in *The Distaff Side* by John Van Druten. After a preliminary discussion with Baxter Somerville, Henson Infield and Francis Donne visited the Croydon theatre and formed a favourable view of the Company playing there. The Directors therefore gave Baxter Somerville a lease of the theatre for three months from 4th February 1935. The first £100 of each week's takings were to go to Somerville, the next £185 to the landlord company, the next £10 to Somerville and any surplus above that amount was to be divided equally between them. The landlord company retained the revenue from the bars, the curtain advertisements and the sale of programmes.

The season proved an artistic but not a financial success, but the tenancy was continued until 4th August, when the Repertory Company went on holiday till 30th September, and thereafter until Christmas.

The Directors than entered into negotiations with both Baxter Somerville and the impresario and former actor, Laddie Cliffe, about renting the theatre for a longer period. However, as an interim measure they gave a lease of the theatre to Andrew Melville. This was originally intended only for a pantomime season of four weeks with Margaret Bannerman and Dan Leno Junior in *Puss in Boots*. But it was actually prolonged until 4th April 1936. Melville introduced a third weekly matinée and at one time even produced twice-nightly shows, like the Hippodrome. This properly upset Lawson Lambert who, knowing the precariousness of his tenure, said that he did not think it worth his while to continue in office during this temporary period without adequate assistance. He had to be mollified with the offer of £1 a performance for every matinée above two that were given in a single week.

Andrew Melville's show was spoiled by the death of King George V on 20th January 1936, when the theatre had to be closed for a week. A loss of £393 14s. 9d. was incurred on the running of the theatre for the whole year.

When Andrew Melville's season finished on 4th April 1936 Lawson Lambert's period as Manager also ended. As far as the Directors of the theatre are concerned his retirement took place in complete silence. There is no expression in the Directors' minutes of any regret that his engagment had to be terminated on account of adverse circumstances, of appreciation of his services during his twenty-eight years in office or of gratitude for the work done by him and the excellent profits earned for the shareholders during the years of prosperity. This reflects little credit on the then Directors, John Henson Infield, George Francis Donne and C. Bruce Seton,[1] who had succeeded Henry John Nye Chart II as a Director in 1934.

Lawson Lambert's services were not, however, overlooked by

[1] His address was the same as one of the original Directors of the company, Jean Ignace Verdié, namely St. Helens Lodge, Hove.

the town of Brighton or by the theatrical profession as a whole. On Tuesday 24th March 1936 a special matinée in his honour was held in the theatre. This seems to have been principally organised by the Managers of the other Brighton theatres, the Hippodrome, the Palace Pier and the West Pier. The broadcaster Christopher Stone, who then lived at Wiston, near Steyning, acted as the compère for the twenty items which comprised the programme. The speech of appreciation was made by Julia Neilson, the widow of Fred Terry. She had known Lambert since he had been at the Brixton Theatre from 1896 to 1903 and over many years had appeared at the Brighton theatre with her husband in all their great successes: *Sweet Nell of Old Drury, The Scarlet Pimpernel, Henry of Navarre*, and *The Wooing of Kartherine Parr*. She spoke of Lambert's courtesy and distinction of manner, which were his outstanding characteristics. John Martin Harvey, who was also of her generation, recited a *Chant of Love for England*. Owen Nares represented the next generation. From the music-hall theatre came Arthur Riscoe, Elsie and Doris Waters, 'Monsewer' Eddie Gray and Dan Leno Junior. William Boland, Margaret Bannerman and Frederick Gregory represented Musical Comedy. At the end of the performance Lawson Lambert himself appeared on the stage with the Mayor of Brighton, Councillor Edward Denne, who presented him with a substantial cheque from his admirers. This did not include the staff of the theatre, who had already made their own presentation to him on a separate occasion.

Baxter Somerville included a generous tribute to Lambert in the first programme of the Repertory Company's second season. He wrote that, during their first season, the Company had felt that Lambert's long experience, profound judgement of character, courage and kindness in moments of difficulty and crisis were continually behind them. 'What you were so fond of quoting about a fellow-manager of yours was profoundly true of you — that the greater the difficulty, the more exasperating the deadlock, the calmer and stronger you were'.

After these tributes we lose sight of Lawson Lambert. But he survived for some years. He continued to live in Palmeiral Mansions, Hove, until at least 1939. He seems to have moved away from here when the war came. He would only have been 65 in 1940.

CHAPTER VII

JOHN BAXTER SOMERVILLE, 1936—1963

JOHN BAXTER SOMERVILLE, or J. B. as he was always called, was quite a different kind of man from Lawson Lambert. He had none of Lambert's panache or grand manner but he was, or rather became, no less a man of the theatre. He was born at Lee in Kent on the 2nd June 1907. His parents were Robert Baxter and Hannah Maude Somerville. He was educated at St. Lawrence's School, Ramsgate, where perhaps he acquired a liking for Regency towns. In due course he qualified as a solicitor and practised as such in London. His firm as Faithful, Owen, Wright and Armstrong, of No. 2 Caxton Street, Westminster, and later of Dacre House, Victoria Street, S.W.1.

He 'entered the theatrical profession', to use the words of *Who's Who in the Theatre*, as publicity director for the Greyhound Theatre, Croydon, in 1931 but did not relinquish his legal practice. He later became the press representative for the Greater London Players and the Little Theatre at Epsom. His first important step in the theatre was the foundation, in 1932, of the Croydon Repertory Company. Two years later he took a lease of the Westminster Theatre for a season of repertory. This theatre had been opened in 1930 by Alderson Burrell Horne whose professional name was Anmer Hall. Baxter Somcrville retained some connection with Anmer Hall for several years, and the latter even made a small appearance in the story of the Theatre Royal, Brighton.

During the year 1934, when touring companies were becoming scarce, Lawson Lambert brought Baxter Somerville's company from Croydon to Brighton for two separate appearances. This was Baxter Somerville's introduction to the Theatre Royal. There could be little doubt that it offered more interesting theatrical prospects than Croydon. He therefore made an offer to lease the theatre. In view of the difficulties that had been experienced booking touring companies during the preceding year the Directors were glad to consider the prospect of a repertory season.

Though the first lease was only for three months, it is clear that Baxter Somerville was thinking in terms of a longer season. To provide support and publicity for the Repertory Company a Repertory Association was therefore formed. The Secretary was Margaret Masterman, a novelist and wife of a Cambridge philosophy don, R. L. Braithwaite. She also acted as stage manager and for short time as manager of the theatre after Lawson Lambert retired. The Treasurer of the Assoication was a young Brighton man who had always been interested in the theatre and, as soon as he knew that a repertory company was being formed, went along to the Theatre Royal to enquire whether he could be of any help. His name was Jack Keates. This was the beginning of twenty-seven years' association with the Theatre Royal. When Margaret Masterman became Manager he was appointed as her assistant and the next year succeeded her as Manager. This post he held until 1963.

The Association was launched at a meeting in the theatre on Saturday 2nd February 1935 at 5.30 p.m., immediately after the matinée performance. The chair was taken by Alderman Miss Margaret Hardy, Deputy Mayor of Brighton and previously Brighton's first woman Mayor. Speeches were made by Baxter Somerville and by Leon M. Lion, who was playing in *Libel* by Ward Doraine at the theatre that week. Telegrams of good wishes were read from Professor, as he then was, J. M. Keynes, and from Violet and Irene Vanbrugh, John Gielgud and Balliol Holloway. The whole of the new Repertory Company who were to act in the theatre the following week were present. The subscription of the Association was 3s. 0d. for three months, for which subscribers were entitled to six vouchers giving them a reduction on the price of seats. A magazine named *Theatre Royal* was issued by the Association. Nine hundred people became members by the end of March 1935. and one thousand five hundred by the same date a year later.

The first performance of the new Company was given on Monday 4th February 1935. The price of seats was 5s. 0d. and 3s 6d.

for the stalls, 4s 0d. and 2s. 6d. for the dress circle, 2s. 6d. and 2s. 0d. for the upper circle, 1s. 6d. for the pit and 10d. for the gallery. Women's headgear was still a matter of concern in the programme, and it was stated that 'hats are not allowed at evening performances'. In fact the word 'bonnets' was still being used in the programme of 1922. Smoking was permitted in the auditorium for the first time. The play was a charming romantic comedy named *Touch Wood* by Dodie Smith, who then wrote under the name of C. L. Antony. The scenery was painted by Bernard Miles. This play was a Scottish and slightly less poignant version of Dodie Smith's Austrian romance *Autumn Crocus*. The first night was quite an artistic and social event in Brighton. Evening dress was worn in the stalls and boxes. The Mayor of Brighton, Councillor S. G. Gibson, attended more or less officially. But this constituted a cheap form of municipal support, especially as the Mayor probably did not pay for his ticket! At no time, not even in the greatest theatrical crisis, did Brighton Council ever give the theatre or its company a penny of financial help.

The Brighton Company was headed by Peter Hoar who directed most of the plays presented. The main Company comprised: Rosamund Barnes, Oliver Burt, Erik Chitty, Tina Dewsnap, Philip Howard, Angela Kirk, Jean Moncrieff, Gwen Nelson, Frank Newman, Cicely Paget-Bowman, Mary Payne, Douglas Seale and Tony Wickham-Jones. The juvenile leads were usually played by Cicely Paget-Bowman or Angela Kirk for the women and Philip Howard or Douglas Seale for the men. The older parts generally fell to Gwen Nelson and Erik Chitty.

Repertory companies are always nurseries of talent, and this was certainly true of the Brighton Company. Cicely Paget-Bowman has had a successful London career, which extends to a fairly long entry in *Who's Who in the Theatre*. Gwen Nelson went on from Brighton to the Birmingham Repertory Company and then to the West End, where she is still playing telling parts. She has made several return visits to the Theatre Royal at Brighton, the most recent occasion being during the week of 2nd May 1977, when she played Aunt Juliana Tesman in *Hedda Gabler*. On the occasion of the Brighton theatre celebrating its hundred and fiftieth anniversary she wrote to Baxter Somerville that the

Plate 14.
The first repertory company.
(from the Theatre programme of 1935.)
(Reproduced by kind permission of the Directors of Brighton Theatre Royal Limited.)

members of the original Repertory Company had always considered their season in Brighton 'the very happiest job of their lives'. Erik Chitty also made at least one return visit and was often to be seen in television plays until his death in 1977. Douglas Seale, after a post war season at the Shakespeare Memorial Theatre at Stratford-on-Avon, became a theatrical director and has made his mark as such.

After the company's first week the succeeding plays were *Three Cornered Moon* by Gertrude Tonkonogy, *Bird in the Hand* by John Drinkwater and *The Maitlands* by Ronald Mackenzie. The season was extended from the original three months until the beginning of August, when the company went on holiday, and was resumed from 30th September until Christmas. In the second phase Richard Wattis and Ronald Waldman joined the company. The former became a well-known film actor, rather type-cast as a stage silly ass. He died quite young. The latter went on to be a dramatic producer for the BBC. He died in 1978.

During the first three months of 1936 Andrew Melville presented a season of pantomime and other plays. During this period a non-profit making company was formed named Community Theatres (Brighton) Limited and registered with the Registrar of Friendly Societies. Its authorised capital was 300 redeemable preference shares of £5 each and 3,500 ordinary shares of £1 each, but it is almost certain that nothing like this sum was ever subscribed. The Chairman was H. B. Chaplin Baldwin of St Andrew's, Montefiore Road, Hove, a well-known Brighton accountant and partner in the firm of E. C. Baldwin and Son. Baxter Somerville was the Managing Director. His address was then given as No. 40 Marine Parade, Brighton. The other Directors were Anmer Hall, who had been associated with Baxter Somerville in the Westminster Theatre, London, Margaret Masterman of 58 Bateman Street, Cambridge and Charles Walker of Eskdale, Old Shoreham Road, Hove, who ran the local firm of Pipes Limited and was Chairman of the National Federation of Builders' Merchants. The Secretary was Chaplin Baldwin's partner, O. O. Dawe.

The new company was given a new lease of the theatre for one year from 11th April 1936 at a rent of £48 a week, with an option to continue for a further period of two years at £50 a week and for four years after that at £55 a week. This included the advertising of the curtain and the programmes. The landlord company was given the right to nominate a representative to serve on the Board of the tenant company. Anmer Hall acted as guarantor of the lease on behalf of the tenants.

The second season of the Repertory Company began on 11th April 1936 with the performance of *Espionage* by William Hackett. The position at the theatre at this time was really a reversion to the time of Henry John Nye Chart. The repertory company was the modern, though supierior, equivalent of the old stock company. This was from time to time augmented by the appearance of a single London star for a special play. For instance, it was joined by Jean Forbes Robertson for Barrie's *Mary Rose* and Shaw's *St Joan*, and by Kenneth Kent to play the part of Napoleon in *St. Helena* by R. C. Sherriff and Jeanne de Casalis. On one occasion Anmer Hall, who acted under the separate stage name of Waldo Wright, made a special appearance as the Dean in Pinero's *Dandy Dick*. The was in contradistinction to the first season when the Company, without outside aid, was not even daunted by *Hamlet*, and Douglas Seale gave a very creditable performance as the Prince.

As in Nye Chart's time, local operatic societies occasionally leased the theatre for a week. In addition there were a few appearances of prior-to-London productions. These seem to have been mainly productions presented by Anmer Hall. The first of these was a play by G. A. Thomas called *Winter Sunshine*, in which Nicholas Hannen acted the part of a blind man who played a confidence trick on one of the women passengers (Athene Seyler). Another such production came nine months later, when Sybil Thorndike and Lewis Casson appeared in a play by Miles Malleson and H. Brooks about the Tolpuddle martyrs named *Six Men of Dorset*. During the six weeks from the end of July to the middle of September, while the company was on holiday, touring companies were brought to the theatre.

During this second season four stage figures of note joined the repertory company. The first, in May 1936, was Penelope Dudley Ward, daughter of King Edward VIII's friend, Mrs Winifred

Dudley Ward. She came from the Liverpool Repertory Company. One of her first parts was Elizabeth Bennet in *Pride and Prejudice*. The second, in July, was Alec Clunes. The third in November, was Judy Campbell, who fairly soon afterwards played the part of Kathy in *Wuthering Heights*. All these three players very soon graduated to London and made a considerable success in the West End and in films, though Alec Clunes died relatively young. The fourth person of note at this time was William Douglas Home who, in March 1937, appeared in *Anthony and Anna* by St John Ervine. He remained with the Company for only a very short period and indeed did not make a name as an actor. But after the war he became a successful dramatist, writing the serious play *And Now Barabbas!* and the comedies *The Chiltern Hundreds, The Reluctant Debutante, The Iron Duchess, The Jockey Club Stakes, Lloyd George Knew My Father*, and more recently *The Kingfisher*. He did actually make a return to the stage in Brighton when one of his plays *Aunt Edwina* visited the theatre during the week of 8th February 1960 and he played a part in it.

The second repertory season ended in July 1937. It had been an artistic success. St John Ervine, who was then the dramatic critic of *The Observer*, made a tour of repertory companies during that summer and reported that the Brighton Company was as good as any which he had seen during his tour but was less civilly treated by the public and the municipality than some repertory companies in other smaller seaside towns. In other words its position was still precarious and, in spite of a good theatrical record, it was not a financial success. At the end of the season £96 in arrears of rent were owing to the landlord company, though the latter had actually made a profit of £1,308 14s. 4d. on the year's running for 1936, instead of a loss of £393 14s. 9d. on the previous year. This enabled them to pay a dividend of 1¼% on their ordinary shares.

The times were still very unfavourable for the theatre as a whole. At the moment of the coronation of King George VI in June 1937 no less than twelve London productions ended their runs during a single fortnight. But this did not prevent Baxter Somerville launching out to present plays in other places than Brighton. Together with Peter Hoar, who had directed the plays produced by the Brighton Repertory Company, he formed another company known as Associated Theatre Seasons Limited. This company presented plays at the Arts and Festival Theatre at Cambridge, in which Baxter Somerville had an interest, and at the Theatre Royal, Norwich, as well as at Cromer and in Jersey. The Brighton Company took a turn at these theatres and did not return to Brighton until the middle of November 1938, by which time its cast was entirely different.

Community Theatres (Brighton) Limited was swiftly in financial difficulties owing to the lack of capital. H. B. Chaplin Baldwin died within a year of the formation of the company. At about the same time the other Directors resigned, leaving Baxter Somerville with the sole responsibility and several thousand pounds' worth of debts. He was even left without anyone to countersign cheques on the small remaining bank balance. He and Kack Keates were therefore forced to carry on the theatre on their own financial responsibility and without salary. Eventually they were able to induce the creditors to agree to a moratorium and to accept a bond for a proportion of the debts due to them while a new Company was formed. The principal figure in this new Company was a Brighton solicitor named Guy Charles Wallington, partner in the firm of J. C. Buckwell and Wallington of No. 70 Grand Parade, Brighton. The new Company, which was known as Theatre Royal (Stage Plays) Limited was also non-profit making and was registered with the Registrar of Friendly Societies, as the old one had been. It had a working capital of only £80. The Chairman was Guy Wallington, the Managing Director Baxter Somerville and the Secretary Jack Keates. I have not been able to ascertain the names of the other Directors as the memorandum and articles of association have not survived. Support built up gradually for the new company, and on 11th March 1938 a special matinée, organised by Walter Giles, was held in the theatre to raise a Theatre Royal endowment fund. Hermione Baddeley, Marie Ney, Derek Oldham, and Lea Seidl gave their services for this. There is no record of the amount raised by this function.

A fresh lease of the theatre was granted early in 1938 to the new company at the rent of £50 a week for two years and thereafter £55 a week. If the rent remained unpaid for seven weeks the landlord company could re-enter into possession of the theatre. Redecoration was needed, and the landlords lent the tenants £500 at 5% interest to carry this out.

With the resident company of actors playing at Baxter Somerville's other theatres he returned to the policy that had been normal for the Brighton theatre in Lawson Lambert's time, namely touring companies and London productions. Donald Wolfit made a visit in March 1938 in *Cyrano de Bergerac* by Edmond Rostand. Perhaps the most notable modern play to appear at this period was Noël Coward's *Design for Living* with Diana Wynyard, Anton Walbrook, Rex Harrison and Alan Webb. This was the original London production, though the play had been performed in New York by Lynn Fontanne, Alfred Lunt and Coward himself as far back as 1933. In April 1939 John Martin Harvey made his final appearance in Brighton in *The Only Way* and *The Burgomaster of Stilemonde*. He had first acted there as a star in 1901 and had no doubt appeared much earlier in supporting roles. The last play to be shown in peace time was *The Flashing Stream* by Charles Morgan, with Godfrey Tearle in the leading part.

Unlike the war of 1914–18, the second World War was a very trying period for the theatre as a whole. All the London theatres at first closed and, when they re-opened, were forced to re-arrange the times of performances in order to ensure that these ended by a time officially fixed for the closing of all places of entertainment. In Brighton this was 10 p.m. Performances thenceforward had to begin at 7 o'clock. The closing regulation was subsequently extended by one hour, which enabled the opening time to be changed to 7.30 p.m. The theatre was closed for only one week during which arrangements for a black-out were made. The play which was cancelled, *A Quiet Wedding* by Esther McCracken, was actually shown a few weeks later. On 11th September the doors were re-opened for *They Walk Alone* by Max Catto.

At first the theatrical position in Brighton was not unfavourable. The town was full as it was a reception area. Moreover, as most London theatres closed at least temporarily and massive aerial bombardment was daily expected, London companies were pleased to take to the road. In fact, exactly a month after the outbreak of war (3rd October) the Theatre Royal saw as spectacular a production as has ever come to Brighton. This was the complete London cast of *The Importance of Being Earnest* with Edith Evans, Peggy Ashcroft, Margaret Rutherford, Gwen Ffrangcon-Davies, John Gielgud, Jack Hawkins and George Howe. The following week Donald Wolfit brought *Hamlet, Macbeth, Twelfth Night, The Merchant of Venice* and *The Taming of the Shrew*. Two weeks later (24th October) saw a play which had had an exceptionally long run in London: *Dear Octopus* by Dodie Smith, with Marie Tempest, Leon Quartermaine and Valerie Taylor. Only John Gielgud from the original cast was missing. His part was played by Hugh Sinclair. After this the Vic-Wells Ballet, with Robert Helpmann and Margot Fonteyn, made a visit of two weeks. *Dear Octopus* and the Vic-Wells Ballet both made return visits in March 1940.

The Christmas show for three weeks was a production which Ivor Novello had specially put on the road to give employment to a company of actors in a difficult period. This was his own comedy *Second Helping*, in which Isobel Jeans, Dorothy Dickson and he himself played the chief parts. It was preceded by a programme of songs called *Song Parade*, sung by Olive Gilbert and Flora Neilson. One of these was his own popular patriotic song entitled *We'll remember the Meadows*, which he hoped would make the same kind of hit in the second World War that *Keep the Home Fires Burning*, composed in his teens, had made in the First War. But it never caught on.

The first performance of 1940 was given by the first touring production that Glyndebourne Opera had ever sponsored. This was *The Beggar's Opera*, with Audrey Mildmay, wife of John Christie, as Polly Peachum and Michael Redgrave as Macheath. Following this week, on the afternoon of Sunday 21st January, John Gielgud gave a lecture-recital in the theatre entitled *Shakespeare in Peace and War* in aid of the Sussex Society for Polish Relief, of which the Chairman was Lady Leconfield, wife of the Lord Lieutenant of the county. The last of the outstanding productions that winter was during the week of 1st April when Irene Vanbrugh, Ernest Thesiger, Cecil Trouncer and Herbert Lomas appeared in Shaw's *In Good King Charles's Golden Days*.

Such an excellent programme did not however exhaust Baxter

Somerville's activities at this period. He also promoted a series of concerts for children at 11 o'clock on a Saturday morning, conducted by the composer, John Greenwood, who lived in Roedean Terrace, Brighton, as well as one similar Sunday evening concert for adults on 12th May 1940. Meanwhile Somerville was also promoting plays in other towns. In the programme of 19th February 1940 he included a note to the effect that, with several companies of about twenty actors each, he had presented no less than one hundred and fifty nine separate show in different places including Brighton and Croydon. These were as far afield as Streatham Hill, Golders Green, Birmingham, Oxford, Norwich, Hull, Huddersfield, Manchester, Liverpool, Southport, Newcastle-on-Tyne, Cardiff, Edinburgh, Glasgow and Dublin.

All this teeming activity and considerable success was cut short by the fall of France during the summer of 1940. The whole situation was immediately transformed. The evacuees from London were hastily removed to other parts of the country. The whole of the south-eastern region of England was declared a restricted area. No one from outside was allowed to enter it without a permit from the Regional Controller, and such was granted only for urgent personal reasons. All the big hotels except the Old Ship in Brighton and the Dudley in Hove were closed to guests and occupied by the armed services as training establishments. Theatrical companies largely ceased to tour. Many London theatres again closed, and there were only two straight plays running in London during July. To keep the theatre open Baxter Somerville's only resort was to improvise an entertainment of concert-party character. The months of July and August therefore saw a season of *Jimmy Hunter and His Brighton Follies*.

This was followed on 9th September 1940 by a return to repertory. Of the original company, the only member to come back to Brighton for this third season was Angela Kirk. With the *Brighton Follies* vanished a feature of the theatre that had existed since before Henry John Nye Chart's time and probably since the theatre was first built, namely the orchestra. This had always played for fifteen minutes before the curtain rose and during the interval. The selection of what they were going to play was printed in the programme. The orchestra-pit remained unoccupied until touring companies again appeared in the theatre in January 1941, when Roy Langridge and Douglas Addey at two pianos took the place of the orchestra and their selection was again printed in the programme.

Douglas Addey had come to the theatre as an art student to help paint the scenery. One day quite by chance he happened to play a piano that was standing by and revealed such talent that Baxter Somerville asked him to stay on as a pianist. Soon afterwards Roy Langridge was replaced by Mary Hargreaves, whom Somerville had found playing the piano in the Palace Pier Theatre before this closed. She and Douglas Addey were later married. They continued to play at the theatre until shortly after the death of Baxter Somerville in 1963. They were then replaced by a single pianist named Hero de Rance and from 1967 onwards by Hazel Dorling, who is still playing at the theatre today.

But returning to 1940, the *Brighton Follies* had not been very successful and the theatre was already in financial difficulties when the Repertory Company opened their third season. The programme of the first week included a word of support from the Mayor of Brighton, Councillor John Talbot Nansen, and an appeal from Baxter Somerville for patrons to buy at least one seat a week each. The play performed during the first week was *Without the Prince* by Philip King. The total takings were only £42. The title of the next week's play fitted the occasion. This was J. B. Priestley's *Dangerous Corner*. The takings were still only £52. But the company struggled on. However, by the middle of October the position was desperate. Several hundred pounds in rent were owing to the landlord company. Salaries had to be cut to the minimum. Often they were not paid in full on a Friday night, and payment of the balance had to be deferred to Monday. The management took no salary at all. To save costs students from the School of Art in Grand Parade were enlisted to design and paint the sets.

During the week of 15th October 1940, when the Company was playing *The Passing of the Third Floor Back* by Jerome K. Jerome, an appeal over the signature of Jack Keates was inserted in the programme to the effect that, if the management could not secure a guaranteed income of £100 a week, the theatre would have to close at the end of the current week. He appealed to patrons to make advance bookings of £1 a week each, namely seven 3s. 0d. stalls or their equivalent, and, if they were not able to make use of the seats themselves, to give them to members of the armed forces who were then stationed in Brighton. He mentioned in his letter that, out of the thirty-four members of the staff of the theatre (apart from the Repertory Company itself), so many had been employed there for a long period that their total length of service amounted to 486 years. The senior member of the staff was Mrs Violet Helliwell, née Russell, whose father had been in charge of the bars. She also started her career in that department but later became a programme-seller, in which role she was well known to all regular patrons of the theatre. By that date she had already been connected with the theatre for fifty years. She actually went on to notch up sixty-three years' service and only retired through ill health in 1953. At that time Baxter Somerville inserted a note about her in the theatre programme, and her friends in the theatre contributed a sum of money with which a televison set was bought and presented to her.

This, however, is to anticipate and, returning to 1940, the sum of £100 for which Jack Keates appealed was not quite raised. But the theatre did not close. In the following week, when *Peg O' My Heart* by J. Hartley Manners was played, a list of names was published in the programme of those who had responded to the appeal for advance booking. This was headed by the Mayor of Brighton, who was amongst those to have given the amount requested. The total came to £68 8s. 6d. The company battled on, and on 5th November things improved with the production of *Pygmalion*, when the takings were three times the amount of those during the first week of the season. Baxter Somerville recorded with gratitude that one lady brought a party of twenty members of the forces each week, and another gentleman insisted on paying a guinea for his 3s. 0d. stall each week.

The Christmas show was *Charley's Aunt* by Brandon Thomas. It was a snowy week, and I well remember attending a performance when there were probably not fifty people in the theatre. The following week of 7th January 1941 saw the end of the Repertory Company in *Love All* by Dorothy Sayers, and indeed the end of repertory in Theatre Royal until the present time. £1,276 10s. 0d. was owing in rent to the landlord company at this time. This four months' season was probably the saddest period in the theatre's annals, or at least the most unfortunate time since Henry Farren had defaulted in 1854.

By the beginning of 1941 the theatrical world seems to have adjusted itself to the abnormal conditions of life in wartime. H. M. Tennant Limited and other managements had put some shows on the road. Therefore Baxter Somerville felt able to return to the pre-repertory practice of the theatre, which had been the normal custom since Mrs Nye Chart's time, of booking a different company every week or fortnight. This has, in fact, remained the practice of the theatre ever since, with the exception of an occasional summer season for a show of concert-party type in July and August. The first play of this new season was *No Time for Comedy* by S. N. Behrman with Diana Wynyard, Rex Harrison and Lillie Palmer. As long as the war lasted there were perhaps not quite as many exceptional productions as had been shown during the period from September 1939 to April 1940. Nevertheless some outstanding companies made appearances. For instance the Sadlers Wells Ballet came in March 1941 and its Opera Company in April with *La Traviata*, *The Marriage of Figaro* and *The Beggars' Opera*, with Joan Cross playing the lead. The week of 30th September 1941 saw a notable performance of *The Cherry Orchard* with Athene Seyler as Madame Ranyerskaia and O. B. Clarence in the telling part of the footman, Firs, who is left behind in the house in the last act. In December Donald Wolfit brought *Hamlet*, *Richard III* and *The Merchant of Venice*. On matinée days, which were then on Wednesday as well as Thursday and Saturday, he performed the stupendous feat of playing the principal part in each of these plays twice on the same day.

During the week of 14th September 1942 there was an innovation in that no play was performed in the theatre but, instead, the Bournemouth Philharmonic Orchestra gave a concert each night. At the six concerts there were five different conductors: Charles Hambourg, Richard Austin, Anatole Fistoulari, Reginald Goodall (twice), and Clarence Raybould, and six soloists: Moura Lympany, Albert Sammons, Eileen Joyce, Moiseivitsch, Pouishnoff and Maria Douska. As a complete contrast the show of two months later was a *Gigantic Circus*. Eileen Joyce came again to the theatre to give a piano recital at 6.30 p.m. on a Sunday evening, 14th March 1943.

The week of 15th December 1942 brought a great wartime play in *Watch on the Rhine* by Lilian Hellman with Zena Dare, Ursula Jeans and Roger Livesey. Another such play named *Tomorrow the World* by James Gow and Arnaud D'Usseau with Jean Cadell came on 21st August 1944. On 4th December the Imperial Opera Company made a visit with *Faust* and *Madame Butterfly*. On 16th April 1945 Anne Casson played the title role in *St Joan*, and on 28th May John Mills made one of his rare appearances on the stage in a gruesome play called *Duet for Two Hands* written by his wife, Mary Hayley Bell.

Throughout the war ballet was well represented at the theatre as there were frequent visits by the Vic-Wells Company, the Ballet Rambert, the Ballet Joos, the Anglo-Polish Ballet and once the Russian Ballet with Lydia Kyasht. On 21st January 1946 Donald Wolfit made a week's visit with seven Shakespeare plays. In addition to his usual *Hamlet*, *Othello*, *The Merchant of Venice* and *Twelfth Night* he added to his repertoire *The Merry Wives of Windsor*, *Cymbeline* and *King Lear*, in which he gave probably his finest Shakespearean performance. The provincial theatre during these war and immediately post-war years owes an immense debt to Wolfit. The strain of eight such performances a week must have been tremendous, when one remembers that an actor of his status in a company such as the National or the Royal Shakespeare Company at Stratford-on-Avon today would rarely be called upon to give more than four such performances in a single week.

Even the war did not prevent Baxter Somerville engaging in other theatrical ventures outside Brighton. He was the Chairman and Honorary Director of Mobile Entertainments (for the armed forces) in the Southern Area. Together with Peter Hoar, who had been the first Director of the Brighton Repertory Company, he promoted a season of plays by Bernard Shaw. This Shaw company came to the Brighton theatre twice: on 6th Octoer 1942 for a fortnight with *Pygmalion*, *Candida*, *Major Barbara*, *Man of Destiny* and *Village Wooing:* and on 21st June with *Arms and the Man*,

Mrs Warren's Profession and *Pygmalion* again.

Baxter Somerville also had the idea of promoting special performances for children at the theatre. This thought probably stemmed from the foundation of the Children's Theatre in London in 1944 by Dr J. J. Warren, the Warden of Toynbee Hall. A year later this venture passed under the management of John and Audrey Christie of Glyndebourne, who had independently sponsored action on the same lines. When Somerville announced his plans the Christies entered into negotiations with him through the Glyndebourne Manager, Rudolph Byng, and Somerville more or less stood aside in favour of the Glyndebourne project. He had, however, interested H. M. Tennant Limited and suggested the Lyric, Hammersmith, as a possible theatre. The result, instead of a children's theatre, was the formation of the Company of Four which promoted plays for four weeks at the Lyric and then for four weeks on tour. This Company provided *Spring 1600* by Emlyn Williams, with Jessica Spencer and Andrew Cruikshank, *Tomorrow's Child* by John Coates and *Thracian Horses* by Maurice J. Valency with Eileen Herlie, which all came to the Brighton theatre during the early part of 1946.

The war years brought a new regime amongst the Directors of the landlord company, Brighton Theatre Royal Limited. C. Bruce Seton had died as far back as July 1937 and had been replaced by C. E. S. Thomas of 20 Liverpool Gardens, Worthing.[1] A more serious loss occurred in January with the death of John Henson Infield, who had been Chairman of the company since 1921. He was succeeded as Chairman by Francis Donne, who held the position for two years until his own death early in 1944. The vacant place on the Board was filled by Henson Infield's nephew, E. Infield Willis, who succeeded him as Chairman of the Southern Publishing Company. When Francis Donne died E. Infield Willis became also the Chairman of Brighton Theatre Royal Limited and held this office until 1961. When the company elected Infield Willis in 1942 they also chose an extra Director. This was Charles James Mackie Whittaker who was Francis Donne's partner in the firm of Nye and Donne, solicitors He also held office until the Board was reorganised in 1961.

[1] He served until his death in 1947.

1947 saw the resignation of C. Knight, an accountant in the Southern Publishing Company, who had acted as Secretary of Brighton Theatre Royal Limited for thirty-five years. He must have been fairly old at the time of his resignation as his handwriting in the minute book became shakier and shakier as the years passed. On 28th November the Directors presented him with a cheque for £50 as a token of their esteem and recognition of his long service. He was succeeded by Miss A. E. Rogers, later Mrs. Thomas, who also became a Director in 1956.

When the war eventually ended the theatre had not only survived without any physical damage but had never closed (other than for the single week compulsorily imposed by the Government in September 1939). It was in full operation and was presenting excellent shows. This well-being was, however, surperficial. Beneath the surface neither of the companies was in a healthy condition. The landlord company, Brighton Theatre Royal Limited, had been forced to impose a moratorium on the payment of interest on its debenture shares as far back as 1942. The Directors were also advised by counsel that the company's preference shares were cumulative preference shares. They had therefore both these sets of arrears to pay off. In fact the last instalment of these arrears was not paid until 1950.

The position of the tenant company, Theatre Royal (Stage Plays) Limited, was even less stable. Though the rent had been reduced to £25 10s. 0d. a week at the most difficult period of the war this was later raised to £40, and a considerable amount was owing. As it was a non-profit making company there was no possibility of appealing to the shareholders for more money. The only possible course therefore was to scrap the company and start again. This is what happened. It seems not to have gone into formal liquidation but just to have faded away.

A new limited liability but private company of the ordinary kind without limitation as to profits was therefore formed. It was registered with the Registrar of Joint Stock Companies on 28th December 1945. By some extraordinary quirk, which may well have been a typist's error not corrected in time, it was registered under the name of Theatre Loyal (Stage Plays) Limited. This was altered to Theatre Royal Brighton (Stage Plays) Limited on 1st

November 1946. The authorised capital was very small: 200 shares of £1 each. On 11th August 1948 this share capital was extended by a further 20 shares of £1 each. We are today so corrupted by inflation that it seems almost impossible to envisage that such a slight increase was worth making. But such was the case at the time.

No less than eight directors were named in the articles of association. These were Guy Charles Wallington, by now a Brighton Councillor, who became Chairman of the new company, as he had been of the old one; Baxter Somerville, who was the Managing Director; Jack Keates, who also acted as Secretary of the company; Major Howard Sydney Johnson, later Member of Parliament for Brighton, Kemp Town Division, who subsequently quarrelled with the other Directors and resigned; Alderman John Talbot Nanson, who as Mayor of Brighton in 1940, had been a good friend to the theatre in sad time; Lewis Coleman Cohen, who succeeded Guy Wallington as Chairman of the company in 1948[1]; Charles Frederick Smith, a rich business man who had founded a Civic Theatre in Leeds and, after he moved to Brighton, was associated with Baxter Somerville in the provision of Mobile Entertainment for the armed forces in the Southern Area during the war; and Captain Lester Grant, a retired journalist and professional soldier with a life-long interest in the theatre.

A fresh lease for seven years had been given to the old company in February 1945 at the rent of £65 a week. This did not run its full course but was replaced by a new lease to the new company for twenty one years from June 1947. The Directors' minutes do not mention the rent to be paid in this last instance. It is this company which has been the tenant of the theatre ever since. But the full details of its history are not as clear as those of the landlord company as its records have been missing since Baxter Somerville's death in 1963.

With these changes effected, both companies set about bringing the theatre back to prosperity. The first important pre-war figure to return to Brighton was Ruth Draper, who had appeared there twice before 1939. She played for a whole week from 22nd April 1946. The sketches which she presented on this occasion were

[1] Guy Wallington resigned through ill health in that year and died in 1949.

Opening a Bazaar, *The Return* (of a prisoner of war), *Doctors and Diets*, *A Debutante* (at a ball) and *In a Church in Italy*.

The first piece of pre-war glamour to be staged in Brighton was the first Regency Festival Exhibition at the Royal Pavilion. This was not, as now, a Corporation activity. It was organised by a group of London people led by Lady Birley of Charleston Manor, West Dean, near Seaford, and Doreen, Lady Brabourne. It was held for a fortnight in August 1946 and was a brilliant success. The Theatre Royal chimed in with the spirit of the Exhibition and during a run of the revue *Twinkle* presented two performances, on 7th and 9th August, of *A Regency Diversion* in the shape of a pastoral opera by Thomas Arne called *Thomas and Sally* or *The Sailor's Return* and two other short operas, *True Blue* by Henry Carey and *Every Maid Her Own Mistress* by Pergolesi. The Regency Society of Brighton and Hove, which had been founded as recently as December 1945, held the first of its lectures in the Royal Pavilion on 29th July, when H. Hamilton Fyffe, the author and journalist, spoke on *The Story of the Theatre Royal*.

The end of the war permitted Baxter Somerville to turn again to other theatrical ventures. The first of these was the purchase in July 1946 of the adjoining Court Theatre in New Road. This had been built in the eighteen-seventies and was originally known as the New Oxford Theatre of Varieties. But it was subsequently called in turn the Brighton Empire, the Brighton Coliseum and the Court Theatre. In May 1947 Somerville re-opened it as a theatre with a performance of *Lot's Wife* by Peter Blackmore, with Nora Swinburne and Richard Bird. He instituted a competition in the programme of the Theatre Royal for yet another new name for the theatre. The largest number of votes were given to the name Regency. But Somerville considered that this presented some difficulties and eventually gave the theatre the name of the competitors' second choice, the Dolphin Theatre. On 16th November 1948 he established a fortnightly season of repertory there. But it did not prosper and had to be discontinued in June 1949. In 1955 the building was converted into a cinema named the Paris, but again failed and was later demolished for redevelopment. It had a fine interior with elaborate plaster-work. At a later period, when Victorian buildings had come to be valued it might well have been listed as a building of special architectural interest and consequently preserved.

At the same period that the Dolphin Theatre was being brought back to life the Stage and Screen Circle was established in Brighton for the benefit of people interested in plays, ballet, theatrical expression of the widest variety and in the best work of the screen. The Chairman was E. Infield Willis, who was Chairman of the Brighton Theatre Royal Limited, and the Honorary Secretary Winifred Ball, but the most active officers were the Vice-Chairman, Charles Smith, who was Director of Theatre Royal Brighton (Stage Plays) Limited, and the Honorary Treasurer, Glynne Burnand, who became a Director of that Company in 1948 and who was a partner in the firm of Burnand and Burnand, solicitors, of 39 Church Road, Hove. The Circle achieved a membership of nearly a thousand. Its aim was to present performances on Sunday evenings at either the Theatre Royal or the Dolphin, but mostly the latter. The first performance was of a Victorian music-hall called *The Late Joys* by the Players Theatre Company at the Dolphin on 16th June 1947. There were several other performances such as *The Young May Moon* by Moira Verschoyle. But the most important was a dramatic recital at the Dolphin by Sybil Thorndike on 23rd October. After a while the Circle quietly expired.

Baxter Somerville's other pre-war company, Associated Theatre Seasons Limited, had either survived the war or was revived afterwards. This controlled the Lyric Theatre, Hammersmith. The Company of Four, which was operated by H. M. Tennant Limited, continued to present plays there. These made their prior appearance at Brighton. Amongst such plays were *The Eagle Has Two Heads* by Jean Cocteau with Eileen Herlie and *Dark Summer* by Wynyard Browne, with Jean Cadell. Wynyard Browne had local connections as he had spent his childhood at Brighton. His father had then been the Vicar of St Mark's Church, Kemp Town.

Several notable plays were produced at the Theatre Royal during 1947. The first of these on 17th February, was *The White Devil* by John Webster with Robert Helpmann and Margaret Rawlings. This is at any time a gruesome play, but its 'realistic' production was perhaps the first of the blood and groans type of presentation that has since unfortunately become all too common. A play of significance in Brighton (April 28th) was *The First Gentleman* by Norman Ginsberg, in which Robert Morley played George IV. Another magnificent play by Arnaud d'Usseau and James Gow, *Deep are the Roots*, about the colour question in the United Sates was shown on 2nd June. In August came the first of the successful comedies by William Douglas Home who had been for a short time in the Brighton Repertory Company in 1937. This was *The Chiltern Hundreds*, with A. E. Matthews as the eccentric Scottish peer, based on the dramatist's father.

April 1948 saw the first appearance in the Brighton theatre of Peter Ustinov, who acted the part of Caligula in the Play *Frenzy* by Ingmar Bergman, which Ustinov had translated and adapted from the Swedish. But as an actor his performance about a year later in *Love in Albania* by Eric Linklater was more important. 13th July 1948 saw the British première of Tennessee Williams's *The Glass Menagerie* with the American actress Helen Hayes.

On 15th November the play was *The Return of the Prodigal* by St John Hankin with Sybil Thorndike, John Gielgud and Rachel Kempson. The part played by John Gielgud had originally been created by A. E. Matthews in 1905. The year ended with Flora Robson in Shaw's *Captain Brassbound's Conversion* on 13th December.

The first notable production of 1949 was a new play by Terence Rattigan about Alexander the Great named *Adventure Story*. In this Paul Scofield made a spectacular success. Scofield was in fact a Brighton man as he was educated at Varndean School for Boys and made his first appearance on stage in the Theatre Royal as part of the revolutionary crowd in Martin Harvey's old play *The Only Way*. The year 1949 brought several other important plays. The first of these on 24th January was *The Heiress* adapted by Ruth and Augustus Goetz from Henry James's novel *Washington Square*, with Ralph Richardson and Peggy Ashcroft. Ralph Richardson also had started his theatrical career in Brighton. His first appearance on the stage was with the Frank Growcott Players at St Nicholas's Hall in December 1920 when he was eighteen. His debut as a professional actor followed nine months later in Lowestoft. *The Heiress* was followed that year by several other productions of importance: on 21st February by Ruth Draper in a much larger repertoire of sketches than she had given in 1946; on 7th March by *The Lady's Not For Burning* by Christopher Fry, with John Gielgud, Pamela Brown, Esmé Percy, Caire Bloom and Nora Nicholson; on 21st March by *Royal Highness,* adapted by Margaret Webster from the play of Felix Salten, in which Judy Campbell and Richard Wattis of the former Repertory Company returned to Brighton; on 19th September by Chekhov's *The Seagull* with Maï Zetterling, Paul Scofield and Isobel Jeans; on 7th November by Benjamin Britten's opera, *Let's Make An Opera* conducted by Norman Del Mar; and on 19th December by the original production of T. S. Eliot's *The Cocktail Party* with Alec Guiness, Cathleen Nesbitt and Robert Flemyng (who at that time was a Brighton resident).

At the beginning of 1950 the theatre was required by the municipal authorities to remove 120 seats on account of new fire regulations. This represented approximately the number of seats that had been added to the auditorium during the alterations of 1927. It was therefore a serious financial blow to the management of such a small theatre, seating only 1,000 people. As a consequence they felt obliged to abolish the unreserved pit, in which the seats were priced at 3s. 0d. each, and to amalgamate it with the stalls, of which the prices at that time were 10s. 6d., 7s. 6d., 6s. 0d. and 4s. 0d. These prices give the measure of inflation since then as, during the single reign of Queen Elizabeth II they have increased sevenfold. The present prices of stalls are £3.25 and £2.75. At the same time as the seats were removed new stage lighting was installed in the theatre.

One of the dominant figures of the theatrical scene in the early nineteen fifties was the French dramatist, Jean Anouilh. Three of his plays, in translation, came to Brighton at about this time: *Ring Round the Moon (L'Invitation au Château)* with Paul Scofield and Margaret Rutherford, on 9th January 1950; *Point of Departure* with Dirk Bogarde, Maï Zetterling and Hugh Griffith, on 23rd October 1950 and *Colombe,* based on the life of Sarah Bernhardt, with Yvonne Arnaud, Esmé Percy and Joyce Redman, on 30th October 1951. Either at this time or later Yvonne Arnaud had a flat in Sussex Square, Brighton. Another feature of this period was the number of film stars who appeared at the theatre. In addition to Dirk Bogarde and Maï Zetterling, who have already been mentioned, there were John Mills in *The Damascus Blade* by Bridget Boland on 20th March 1950, Françoise Rosay in *Madame Tic-Tac* by Falkland Cary and Philip Weathers the following week and Ann Todd with Leo Genn and Herbert Lom in *The Seventh Veil* by Muriel and Sydney Box on 12th February 1951. The play shown during the week of 13th March 1950 subsequently became a successful film. This was the second play written by Wynyard Browne, *The Holly and the Ivy*, with Jane Baxter and Herbert Lomas.

1951 was an outstandingly successful year for the Theatre Royal. No less than three weeks were devoted to Shakespeare, two of them comprising visits by the Old Vic Company. The first of these was *Twelfth Night* on 15th January. Peggy Ashcroft played Viola, Ursula Jeans Olivia, Paul Rogers Malvolio, Roger Livesey Sir Toby Belch, Robert Eddison Sir Andrew Aguecheek, Leo McKern Feste, William Devlin Antonio, Alec Clunes (who had started his stage career in the Brighton Repertory Company) Orsino. Even the minor parts of the Sea Captain and a Page were played by Rupert Davies and Dorothy Tutin respectively. The second Old Vic visit was with *Othello* on 1st October. Douglas Campbell played the Moor. Other prominent members of the cast were Paul Rogers, Irene Worth, Coral Browne, Nicholas Hannen and Ernest Milton. The third Shakespeare play to be seen during the year, but not with the Old Vic Company, was *The Winter's Tale*. This had however, the equally remarkable cast of John Gielgud, Lewis Casson, Diana Wynyard, Flora Robson and Virginia McKenna.

The third Regency Exhibition in Brighton was held during July 1951 as part of the Festival of Britain, 1951. The Theatre Royal's contribution was the production of a play about Gainsborough which Cecil Beaton had written specially for the occasion, *The Gainsborough Girls*, with Angela Baddeley, Muriel Pavlow and Michael Shepley. At the same time an exhibition was arranged in the foyer of the theatre of Regency play-bills from the private collection of Raymond Mander and Joe Mitchenson.

Other notable productions during the year were *Waters of the Moon* by N. C. Hunter on 26th March with Sybil Thorndike, Edith Evans, Kathleen Harrison and Wendy Hiller; *Intimate Relations*, adapted by P. Charles Frank from Jean Cocteau's *Les Parents Terribles*, on 25th June, in which a return to the Brighton stage was made both by Fay Compton, who played the principal part, and by Cicely Paget-Bowman, who had been in the original Brighton Repertory Company; and Emlyn Williams on 22nd October when he gave for the first time his readings from and impersonation of Charles Dickens. Over thirty weeks during this year were devoted to prior-to-London productions. This proportion in fact remained constant for several years in succession.

By the end of 1951 the two theatre companies were not only sucessful dramatically but were also restored to financial stability. The landlord company (Brighton Theatre Royal Limited) had paid the arrears of dividends on its debenture and preference shares in full. In 1951 it declared the first dividend on its ordinary shares since 1940. This was only 1½% that year, but in 1952 and 1953 this was increased to 2½% and later to 4% or 5%, though never again to the 10% that had been normal between 1918 and 1931. From 1952 onwards the company resumed paying its Directors a fee of £150 a year each. In 1952 the Board also managed to pay off the £3,000 capital of the third mortgage debentures which had been issued in 1896 and 1927. The next year they even bought back for £5,900 the Colonnade Hotel (No. 10 New Road), which had been sold for £5,750 in 1935 during the depression.

At about this time two new appointments were made to the Board of Directors. C. E. S. Thomas had died in 1947. In 1949 George Scatliff, partner in the firm of Johnson, Mileham and Scatliff, solicitors of 64 Ship Street, Brighton, was elected in his place. The following year the name of Nye Chart again appears in the annals of the theatre. Henry John Nye Chart II, who had died in 1934, left three sons. None of them went on the stage. The second son, Eric, was killed in the war in 1916, aged 20. The third, Aubrey Vivian Pelham Chart also left no issue. In 1950 the eldest son, Henry Nye Chart III, then of 56 Meadway, Old Southgate, London N.14, became a Director of the Theatre Royal and remained a member of the Board until his death in 1954. He left one son, who is unmarried. Two of his sisters, Mrs Lota Kindersley and Mrs Cynthia Williams, are also living, one of whom has a son. So there are still descendants of the original Nye Chart couple living today.

1952 saw as distinguished a programme as the year before. Prior-to-London productions were played on forty weeks. Three of these were Shakespeare plays, two of them being performed by the Old Vic Company. The first of these was *A Midsummer Night's Dream* on 25th February with much the same cast as in *Othello* the previous year, except for Joan Plowright instead of Coral Browne. The second was *King Lear* on 7th April. William Devlin gave a notable performance as the King. Freda Jackson and Coral Browne played Goneril and Regan respectively and Leo McKern the Fool. The third Shakespeare play but without the Old Vic Company was *Richard II* on 8th December with Paul Scofield, Herbert Lomas and Eric Porter.

Other notable productions were *The Deep Blue Sea* by Terence Rattigan, with Peggy Ashcroft and Kenneth More on 4th February; a revival of Noël Coward's *The Vortex* with Isobel Jeans and Dirk Bogarde on 18th February; another magnificent play by Lilian Hellman, *Montserrat*, on 24th March; an insect play by Sam Spelwack called *Under the Sycamore Tree*, with Alec Guiness and Diana Churchill on 31st March; *The Innocents*, which was a dramatisation by William Archibald of Henry James's novel, *The Turn of the Screw*, with Flora Robson, on 12th May and Shaw's *The Millionairess*, with Katharine Hepburn and Robert Helpmann, on 16th June. On 27th June there was a midnight matinée performance of a revue by the whole cast of the Windmill Theatre, London, in aid of the International Equestrian Fund, in which Baxter Somerville was interested. The compères of the show were Alan Melville and Bill Owen, both of whom were Brighton residents.

1953 began with a performance of *A Woman of No Importance* on 27th January, with Clive Brook, Athene Seyler, Isobel Jeans, Nora Swinburne, Jean Cadell and William Mervyn. Clive Brook then or later occupied a flat in Lewes Crescent, Brighton. In the place of the Shakespeare plays of the two preceding years a company of Old Vic status presented by John Gielgud brought two other classic plays to Brighton during the year. The first of these was Congreve's *The Way of the World* on 9th February, the second *Venice Preserved* by Thomas Otway on 4th May. The cast comprised Gielgud himself, Paul Scofield, Eric Porter, Margaret Rutherford, Eileen Herlie and Pamela Brown. On 6th April John Mills brought another play by his wife, Mary Hayley Bell, named *The Univited Guest.* A fortnight later Noël Coward made his only appearance as a star at the Theatre Royal, playing King Magnus in *The Apple Cart.* The week of 29th June was a special occasion in that it saw the first performance in the theatre by Alfred Lunt andLynn Fontanne of *Quadrille* which Noël Coward had written specially for them. Another landmark, on 26th October, was the appearance of Laurence Olivier and Vivian Leigh in *The Sleeping Prince* by Terence Rattigan. Martita Hunt played the role of the Queen Mother, which was afterwards taken by Sybil Thorndike in the film. Richard Wattis, who had started life in the Brighton Repertory Company, took the part in both the play and the film of the British diplomat who was attached to the Prince Regent of Carpathia. In spite of Laurence Olivier's long later connection with Brighton, he has appeared comparatively seldom at the Theatre Royal. His first professional appearance on the stage after leaving the dramatic school in 1925 was actually in Brighton, but at the Hippodrome. The rarity of his appearances at the Theatre Royal seems due only to the accident that several of the play's in which he starred such as for instance *The Entertainer,* have gone to the Hippodrome instead of to the older theatre.

Wynyard Browne's third play *A Question of Fact,* with Gladys Cooper, Paul Scofield and Pamela Brown was shown on 9th November. The year ended with a performance of *Charley's Aunt.* Quite apart from the fact that the cast included John Mills and Gwen Ffrangcon-Davies, the production was much happier than the occasion when it had been the Christmas play given by the Brighton Repertory Company in 1940.

During this year (1953) a new ventilation system and new electric wiring were installed in the theatre. The entrances and exits to the dressing rooms were also improved. These renovations cost the tenant company, Theatre Royal Brighton (Stage Plays) Limited, £23,000.

In the early part of 1954 two remarkable plays were staged: *The Burning Glass,* which was Charles Morgan's best play, with Faith Brook, Laurence Naismith and Robert Speaight on 23rd March, and *The Dark is Light Enough,* which is probably Christopher Fry's best play, with Edith Evans, on 23rd March. On 3rd May Joyce Grenfell, who could perhaps be described as Ruth Draper's successor, brought her one-woman show *Joyce Grenfell Requests the Pleasure* to the theatre. A week later saw Noël Coward's musical version of *Lady Windermere's Fan* which he called *After the Ball,* with Vanessa Lee, Mary Ellis and Irene Browne. On 30th August Peggy Ashcroft appeared in *Hedda Gabler,* with the great Irish actor Michael Mac Liammoir playing Judge Brack.

Towards the end of the year (22nd November) an unusual incident occurred. The play given was of no special merit: *Accounting for Love,* which had been adapted by Henry Hewes from *La Belle Aventure* by Robert de Flers and Armand Caillavet. But the principal part in it was played by the distinguished Norwegian actor Per Aabel, of the Norwegian National Theatre. The Norwegian Ambassador in London and his wife attended the first night, and a telegram of good wishes was received in the theatre from the King of Norway. But the critic of the *Brighton Herald* took it upon himself to give Per Aabel such an unfavourable notice that Baxter Somerville, in his letter 'You and I' in the theatre programme of the following week, complained that this review exceeded the bounds of all reasonable comment, particularly in the case of a guest actor playing in a language not his own. He was fully justified, as much of the review was crudely irrelevant and the headlines wholly so. But he could have taken comfort from the fact that the review in the *Brighton Gazette* of the same day could not have been more complimentary about Per Aabel's performance.

During the nineteen-fifties Baxter Somerville launched out into further ventures outside Brighton. In 1953 he joined Roy Limbert in reviving the Malvern Festival Company and took a lease of the Pavilion Theatre at Torquay in which to present it. The next year he started an even more interesting enterprise by buying the old Theatre Royal at Margate. This was not quite as old as the Georgian Theatre Royal at Richmond, Yorkshire. It had been built in 1787, though it was altered in 1829 and again in 1879. The exterior dated wholly from the Victorian reconstruction, but the interior was almost entirely of Regency character and is one of the most delightful in the country. The theatre had not been used as such for about fifty years. Baxter Somerville restored and opened it for a season on Twelfth Night 1956. The venture was not, however, successful. After Somerville's death in 1963 the theatre became a cinema and later a bingo-hall. Today there is some prospect of its being re-opened as a theatre.

The first notable theatrical event in Brighton in 1955 was a poetry reading by Margaret Rutherford and Paul Scofield on Sunday 20th March. On 2nd May Dorothy Tutin appeared in Jean Anouilh's play about Joan of Arc, *The Lark*. During June two Shakespeare plays were shown prior to a European tour, in which they were played at Vienna, Zurich, The Hague, Amsterdam and Rotterdam. These were a sparkling production of *Much Ado about Nothing* with John Gielgud and Peggy Ashcroft and a much less successful *King Lear*. The name part was reckoned one of Gielgud's rare failures, but this could hardly be held to have been his fault as the scenery and costumes were designed by the Japanese, Isamu Noguchi, and were so futuristic that they projected the play, not into the remote past, but into a space age and at times introduced unexpected comic incidents into the tragic events. Later in the year (25th October) a third Shakespeare play, also prior to a continental visit, was shown. This was *Hamlet* with a cast including Paul Scofield, Diana Wynyard, Ernest Thesinger, Mary Ure and Alec Clunes. The European performances which followed were at Moscow and Leningrad.

1956 was the centenary of the birth of Bernard Shaw. This was celebrated in no uncertain measure at the Theatre Royal by the production of no less than five of his plays. The first was *Misalliance* on 23rd January, with Roger Livesey, Ursula Jeans and Donald Pleasance; the second *The Doctor's Dilemma* on 18th September with Ann Todd, Lewis Casson and Michael Hordern; then a double bill of *Village Wooing* and *Fanny's First Play* on 2nd October, with Brenda Bruce and Michael Dennison and lastly *The Devil's Disciple* on 29th October with Tyrone Power. Erik Chitty, who had been in the Brighton Repertory Company, played a small part in the last of these plays.

Two other notable events of this year were the first plays of two novelists of distinction. The first of these was *The Power and the Glory* by Graham Greene on 26th March, in which Paul Scofield played the principal part of the relapsed priest. The second had special local connections. This was *The Chalk Garden* on 2nd April, with Edith Evans, Peggy Ashcroft and Felix Aylmer. It was written by Enid Bagnold (Lady Roderick Jones) who lived and still lives at Northend House, Rottingdean, and was inspired by her own garden at that house. The following week saw a play that was to become more famous as a film, namely *Gigi,* dramatised from Colette's novel by herself and Anita Loos, with Leslie Caron, Esmé Percy and Tony Britton.

Early in January another of Noël Coward's new plays, *South Sea Bubble,* was produced at the theatre. On the afternoon of 13th January Peter Katin gave a piano recital. A month later 11th February) Donald Wolfit made one of his rare appearances in a contemporary play: *The Master of Santiago* by Henri de Montherlant. In June the hundred and fiftieth anniversay of the opening of the first theatre in New Road occurred. For some reason or other Baxter Somerville chose not to celebrate it until Sunday 29th July, when he gave a party on the stage. To this he invited all the stars who had appeared on the stage of the theatre during his regime there. Of the original Brighton Repertory Company Gwen Nelson, Cicely Paget-Bowman, Barbara Leake and Stafford Byrne attended. On 9th December the Oxford Playhouse Company presented Dylan Thomas's *Under Milkwood.* The play which ended the year was as unlike the usual Christmas show as it was possible to imagine but was one of the most distinguished productions ever to be staged at the Theatre Royal. This was a visit for three weeks by the Lunts (Lynn Fontanne and Alfred Lunt) in Friedrich Durrenmatt's thrilling but macabre play which was then called *Time and Again* but was later retitled in both the play and the opera that was made from it *The Visit* or *The Old Lady's Visit.* This was the second and last of the two occasions when the Lunts together visited the Brighton theatre.

The first production of interest in 1958 (13th January) was *A Touch of the Sun,* which was probably N. C. Hunter's best play. In this Michael Redgrave made one of his rare visits to the theatre. With him were his daughter, Vanessa, as well as Diana Wynyard and Ronald Squire. A fortnight later Graham Greene's third play *The Potting Shed* was played by John Gielgud, Gwen Ffrangcon-Davies and Irene Worth. On 31st March there was the double bill of *The Dock Brief* and *Shall We Tell Caroline?*, which were the first plays written by John Mortimer. In a programme note at the time Baxter Somerville wrote that Mortimer was 'a new author of whom I confidently prophesy that we shall hear a good deal more'. The leading parts were played by Michael Hordern and Brenda Bruce. Both these actors had Brighton connections. Michael Hordern was educated at Brighton College and, while there, played all Henry Lytton's parts in the Gilbert and Sullivan operas, for the production of which the College was then famous. Brenda Bruce and her husband, Roy Rich, then or later lived at Saxon Lodge, Clifton Place, a very attractive Gothic house which had been built about 1830 and later was used as the Vicarage for St Nicholas's Church, when St Peter's became the parish church. It was sold by them to another actor, Clive Brook, who resold it for demolition. This was a severe architectural loss for Brighton.

An unusual appearance at this time was that of Peter Sellers who played for four weeks during August in a play called *Brouhaha* by George Tabori. T. S. Eliot's second play, *The Elder Statesman*, with Paul Rogers and Anna Massey followed on 8th September. The play acted on 15th December, *The Gilt and the Gingerbread* by Lionel Hale, was not in itself remarkable, but the principal parts were played by John Clements and Kaye Hammond, who were then living at No. 7 Royal Crescent and have remained Brighton residents ever since. The year ended with *Eighty in the Shade*, which had been specially written by Clemence Dane for Lewis Casson and Sybil Thorndike who celebrated their golden wedding during the fortnight's run in Brighton.

The first production in 1959 was Robert Bolt's first play, *The Flowering Cherry*, with Ralph Richardson and Meriel Forbes. The play in which Peggy Ashcroft appeared on 26th January, *The Coast of Coromandel*, was by a Lewes resident J. M. Sadler. On Saturday 14th February Queen Elizabeth II, when staying the weekend with Lord and Lady Rupert Neville at Uckfield House, attended a performace of *Prince Genji* by William Cooper, adapted from a Japanese novel. A week later Princess Margaret, on a similar visit, came to *Wolf's Clothing* by Kenneth Horne. 4th May saw a remarkable partnership in the appearance of Donald Wolfit and Flora Robson in *Ghosts*. On 15th June the Oxford Playhouse Company brought a production of *Twelfth Night* which had been shown in Lisbon the week before and was to make visits in the following weeks to Copenhagen, Rome and Zurich.

At this time Baxter Somerville wrote in his letter 'You and I' in the theatre programme that Brighton was then the only seaside place in the country which housed a different company each week or fortnight. All the other town that still had theatres in operation as such had resident shows during the summer. He found that it was becoming increasingly difficult to book plays as management did not like opening with new plays in London during the summer. This no doubt accounted for the fact that during the summer of 1959 he introduced the *Fol-de-Rols* for a season of eleven weeks.

When the normal pattern was resumed in September Donald Wolfit made another visit in *Landscape with Figures* by Cecil Beaton. This brought the return to Brighton of another actor who knew the Theatre Royal well in the person of Douglas Seale who directed the play and had been in the original Brighton Repertory Company. Another substantial Brighton connection can be noted for the week of 9th November when Anna Neagle appeared in *The More the Merrier* by Ronald Miller. She and her husband, Herbert Wilcox, had long been residents at No. 18 Lewes Crescent, Brighton.

The week of 25th April 1960 saw a remarkable play about industrial relations in Northern Ireland. This was *Over the Bridge* by Sam Thompson. During this year the theatre was to see two outstanding plays by Robert Bolt. The first was *A Man for All Season* with Paul Scofield and Leo McKern, and the second *The Tiger and the Horse* with Michael Redgrave, Catherine Lacey and Vanessa Redgrave. The summer show for five weeks was *The Boy Friend* by Sandy Wilson.

On 12th September Enid Bagnold's play *The Last Joke* was produced with John Gielgud, Ralph Richardson, Ernest Thesinger, Robert Flemyng and Anna Massey. A most attractive innovation, on 17th October, was Podrecca's Piccoli Theatre of Marionettes. On 29th October the Queen paid another visit to the theatre, when the play was *The Bride Goes Back* by Ronald Miller, with Robertson Hare, Jack Hulbert and Cicely Courtneidge. As before, the pattern was repeated in that Princess Margaret and her husband, the Earl of Snowdon, made a similar visit a week later to *Toys in the Attic*, the macabre play by Lilian Hellman, with Diana Wynyard, Coral Browne and Wendy Hiller. On all these occasions the royal party sat in the stalls, and the seats were booked by telephone only a few days beforehand. A French newspaper came out with the extraordinary story that on the occasion of the Queen's second visit to what it called a cinema she had had to stand in a queue in the rain to obtain a ticket! The last notable production of that year was the one-man show by Michael Mac Liammoir of extracts from the works of Oscar Wilde which he called *The Importance of Being Oscar*.

For a fortnight in March 1961 a play by Archibald McLeish was presented with the appropriate title of *J. B.* Donald Sinden, who appeared in it with John Clements, Constance Cummings and Paul Rogers, wrote in the current theatre programme that when he had first been offered the title part he had prepared himself to imitate Baxter Somerville, who was always called 'J. B.', by laying in a stock of sports-coats with leather patches at the elbows and padding to represent Somerville's ample figure, only to discover when he received the script that the part was no less that that of the prophet Job!

On 10th April Noël Coward's new play about actresses in retirement, *Waiting in the Wings*, was shown with Sybil Thorndike, Lewis Casson and Marie Löhr. After herself retiring from the stage Marie Löhr was later to live in Hove and in fact died there. On 5th June the Meadow Players presented *Hamlet* with Jeremy Brett in the title role. On 23rd October *Heartbreak House* was performed by Roger Livesey, Michael Dennison, Dulcie Gray and Judy Campbell. The last interesting event of the year was a Sunday evening recital of ballads, poems and other pieces by Flora Robson on 3rd December.

During 1961 a complete re-organisation took place within the landlord company, Brighton Theatre Royal Limited. Over the years the largest number of shares in this company (783 ordinary shares) had come into the hands of the Southern Publishing Company. In addition its Chairman, who was also Chairman of the Brighton Theatre Royal Limited, or a member of his family, owned another 200 shares. Two other Directors had fairly large holdings: George Scatliff 200 ordinary shares and Charles Whittaker or a member of his family 118 ordinary shares and 75 preference shares. The only other holding of substance was that of Mrs Dorothy Nye Chart, widow of Henry Nye Chart III, who held 134 ordinary and 108 preference shares. The people who actually ran the theatre and were representatives of the other company, Theatre Royal Brighton (Stage Plays) Limited had very small holdings: Baxter Somerville only 30 shares and Jack Keates 20 shares. In fact, as recently as October 1950 the Board of the landlord company had recorded in their minutes that they wished to retain absolute control of the company and 'to circumvent, if possible, any further transfer of shares to the tenant company'.

In November 1961 the Theatre Royal Brighton (Stage Plays) Limited, which was by then prosperous, made an offer to acquire all the shares in the landlord company at the price of £15 per ordinary share and £10 per preference share. This offer was not accepted, though no reason for the refusal was given in the minutes. The circumstances suggest that the Directors did not consider that the offer was good enough. Eight months later Theatre Royal Brighton (Stage Plays) Limited did in fact acquire what was virtually the whole share capital of the landlord company. It is not possible to specify the exact price per share which was paid as only the total sum paid is given in the minutes, and this does not discriminate between preference and ordinary shares. But it seems likely that the price paid for the ordinary shares was about £18 a share. Baxter Somerville retained one share, presumably to give him the right to attend the annual meeting of the company. He was not a Director of the landlord company, but at the same time the articles of association of that company were altered to make it unnecessary for the Directors to hold any share qualification. All the existing Directors resigned. These were E. Infield Willis (Chairman), Charles Whittaker, George Scatliff and Mrs A. E. Thomas, who was also Secretary of the Company. She was paid £300 compensation for loss of office, and all the Directors were granted the right of free seats in the theatre (against adequate notice) for the period of twenty-one years or for the duration of their lives, whichever might be the shorter.

The new Directors were the Directors of the tenant company, Theatre Royal Brighton (Stage Plays) Limited, namely Lewis C. Cohen, Chairman; M. G. Burnand, who has already been mentioned in connection with the Stage and Screen Circle and who had been a Director of the tenant company since 1948; A. E. Brocke and A. E. Russell. Albert Brocke was a retired business man who was an Alderman of Hove and had been Mayor of that Borough from 1951 to 1954. A. E. Russell was an accountant of Russell, Ohly and Company of No. 94 Church Road, Hove. Henceforward he assumed responsibility for the financial affairs of the theatre. His firm became the accountants to the both theatre companies, and the registered offices of companies were transferred to No. 94 Church Road. L. H. Elliott of that firm became the Secretary of both companies and still holds this office at the present time. The firm of James Fraser remained for another three years auditors to the theatre, as it had been since the original company was formed in 1889. The new Directors of Brighton Theatre Royal Limited were at first paid salaries of £100 a year each, but in 1962 Lewis Cohen intimated that he did not wish to draw any fees as a Director and henceforward did not do so. In 1963 the other Directors' salaries were increased to £150 a year each and in the following year to £200. From 1962 onwards the tenant company, Theatre Royal Brighton (Stage Plays) Limited, became the dominant company, and the original company, Brighton Theatre Royal Limited, became only a subsidiary company whole role was limited to the ownership of the theatre building.

The new Chairman, Lewis Cohen, who had been Chairman of the tenant company since 1949, played a prominent part in the affairs of the theatre during the next five years. He was born in 1897, the son of Hyam and Esther Cohen, and was educated at Hastings and Brighton Grammar Schools. As we have seen, he started life as an auctioneer and estate agent at No. 14 New Road, Brighton, in 1920. He became Secretary of the Brighton and Hove Building Society (later renamed the Alliance Building Society) in

1929, its Managing Director in 1933 and also its Chairman in 1959. He made a substantial fortune out of property development during the twenties and thirties. He became a Brighton Councillor in 1930 and served as such for thirty-six years. He was a very successful Mayor of Brighton in 1956-7. During his year of office he gave great assistance in the steps leading to the eventual establishment of the University of Sussex in Brighton. His great ambition was to become a Member of Parliament. He stood six times as a candidate for such in the Labour interest: in 1931 and 1935 for the united constituency of Brighton and Hove, in 1950 for Hastings and in 1951, 1955 and 1959 for Brighton, Kemp Town division, but was unsuccessful on all six occasions. However, he eventually arrived in Parliament by another route as in 1965 he was created a Life Peer under the title of Lord Cohen of Brighton. He died on 21st October 1966, aged 68.

The re-organisation of the theatre companies in 1961 did not affect the running of the theatre, but in 1962 outstanding productions were not perhaps as numerous as they had been in the preceding years. The Queen made a third private visit to the theatre on Saturday 14th April. The play was *A Time to Laugh* by Robert Crean with Ruth Gordon, Robert Morley and Cleo Laine. She was not lucky with her choice of play on any of her visits. The most remarkable show of the year was probably John Gielgud's recital *The Ages of Man*, based on George Ryland's Shakespeare Anthology. This was given on 30th April for a whole week. On 22nd October Michael Redgrave appeared in *Out of Bounds* by Arthur Watkyn.

This year was the last year of Baxter Somerville's regime. On 24th September he wrote in the theatre programme: 'If the time ever comes when the grateful citizens of Brighton decide to make a presentation to the Managing Director of their theatre I guess that the most appropriate gift would be either a wig or a large bottle of hair-restorer and plenty of good dye.' He was only 55 years old at the time when he wrote this, and seems not to have realised that he was about to face much worse trials than theatrical worries. Within weeks he fell ill and had to undergo an exploratory operation. Three weeks convalesence at the Palace Court Hotel, Bournemouth, followed, after which he returned to his Brighton flat.

But as the illness was cancer of the lungs the operation provided only a brief respite. He was compelled to re-enter the nursing home at No. 48 Westbourne Villas, Hove, and died there on 19th January 1963. His funeral service was held at St Paul's Church, Brighton, on 28th January. The last production at the Theatre Royal during his life was the two-men show of Michael Flanders and Donald Swann, *At the Drop of a Hat*.

Baxter Somerville's will was dated 19th November 1962. The executors were his legal partner, Alan Wright of Dacre House, Victoria Street, London, Frank Robert Porter, accountant, and Reginald Cornish of the Lyric Opera House, Hammersmith. He left the goodwill of his legal firm to Alan Wright; the lease of the Lyric Theatre and his shares in the company, Associated Theatre Seasons Limited, to Reginald Cornish; the lease of the Paris Cinema, (formerly the Dolphin Theatre), Brighton, to Ann Travers, who is now the manager of the Theatre Royal and was then Somerville's Assistant Manager and also his assistant at the Theatre Royal, Margate; and his farmhouse in Somerset, with its contents, to Cyril and Elizabeth Brick, who acted as its caretakers. The name of this house was Hartrow Manor, Stogumber. One wonders whether, in choosing it, Somerville was in any way motivated by its theatrical connection with John de Stogumber of Shaw's *Saint Joan?* The residue of his estate was to be divided in halves between Reginald Cornish and Cyril and Elizabeth Brick. The gross value of his estate was £36,266 4s. 0d., but it was so encumbered with debts that it is very doubtful whether any of the legatees ever received anything at all from it.

The death of Baxter Somerville was the end of an epoch in the history of the Brighton theatre. When he first appeared on the scene there it would have been difficult to imagine a greater contrast than between him and his predecessor. Lawson Lambert looked and dressed like a member of an aristocratic household, whether baronet or butler. J. B. looked and dressed like a fairly prosperous farmer who had strayed into the theatre after selling his produce in the market. In the daytime he usually wore an old sports coat patched with leather at the elbows and sometimes jodhpers. This perhaps reflected the interest which, with him, was second only to the theatre, namely horses. In the evening on

Plate 15.
"J.B." (John Baxter Somerville.)
Photograph taken shortly before his death in 1963.
(Reproduced by kind permission of Mrs. Winifred Keates.)

the rare occasions, latterly at least, when he wore a dinner jacket, such as when the Queen visited the theatre, this looked as if he had borrowed it for the night.

He had many abodes — homes would be quite the wrong word: a basement flat at No. 17 Lewes Crescent, Brighton (next door to Anna Neagle and Herbert Wilcox); a flat attached to the Dolphin Theatre or Paris Cinema; a flat in London and a farmhouse in Wales, or from 1961 onwards at Stogumber in Somerset. All were in the utmost disarray, the disorder of a bachelor who cared neither for comfort nor even for cleanliness.

He was a man of many contradictions. Trained and qualified as a solicitor, he was yet so unbusinesslike that on many occasions when his financial affairs were in a precarious condition he ignored or neglected an offer to purchase one of his theatres, or some other property with which he was connected that would have lifted him out of all financial difficulty. When he died a drawer in his desk at the theatre was found full of unopened letters, some of them, naturally, bills. One wonders what legal advice he can possibly have given to his clients as a solicitor when his own affairs were so muddled.

This was not his only contradiction. Passionately devoted to animals, particularly horses, he had so little appreciation of their needs that at his farmhouse in Wales, when he was away, he would leave them with a supply of food but no provision for this to be given to them regularly, as if he thought that they were capable of rationing the food out themselves. Though he spent most of his working life in the extrovert world of the theatre, he was himself in some ways so withdrawn that, if he met an acquaintance in the street, he gave the impression of hoping that they would pass on without speaking.

But even in the theatre he seemed sometimes divided in his mind. His great passion was to revive theatres which had gone out of use. But when he had brought them back to life he seemed sometimes to lack the interest to sustain them or had too many irons in the fire to be able to look after them properly and prevent them subsiding once more into oblivion. By that time he was thinking of other sleeping princesses who needed the kiss of life. None of his theatrical ventures outside Brighton, except possibly the Lyric, Hammersmith, had lasting success.

But of the Theatre Royal, Brighton, he never tired — fortunately for the town. To this he was always constant and devoted and his staff in it were equally devoted to him. Here he had tremendous flair in many ways: in choosing, during the days of the Repertory Company, actors and actresses who were to have a promising future in the theatre; in selecting, after the repertory system had been abandoned for visiting companies, the plays and companies which were booked to come to theatre; in establishing good relations with managements so that other shows of theirs were available to his theatre; and in making the stars in these plays at home in the theatre so that they welcomed a week or a fortnight's visit to Brighton. Fortunately both for him and for Brighton he was not directly involved in the financial side of the theatre's affairs. He was paid a salary as the Managing Director of the Theatre Royal Brighton (Stage Plays) Limited but had virtually no shares in it. So the theatre did not become a casualty to his divided financial commitments and lack of good business management.

His achievements were first, that he twice saved the theatre from closing, in the depression years of 1935–6 and the greatest crisis of the war from 1940–1; second, when normality had returned to life, or even before this, he built up the theatre again both dramatically and financially to the prosperity that it had known in the pre-war years under Mrs Nye Chart and under Lawson Lambert, so that it is still today one of the most distinguished provincial theatres in the country. He and Mrs Nye Chart are undoubtedly the greatest figures in the history of the Theatre Royal. Baxter Somerville cannot rival her financial success, but in the purely theatrical sphere his achievement was of very similar quality.

CHAPTER VIII

1963 - 1977

When Baxter Somerville died Jack Keates, who had been Manager of the theatre since 1936, carried on the management for a few weeks. He was immediately made a Director of Brighton Theatre Royal Limited at a salary of £150 a year, which was increased to £200 in 1964. But being eligible for a pension and having served under Baxter Somerville for twenty-seven years, he not unnaturally did not fancy working under a new Managing Director. He therefore retired on the 20th April 1963. He remained a Director of the company until the theatre changed hands in 1971. At the instigation of the Chairman, Lord Cohen, he was allotted 20 shares in the Theatre Royal Brighton (Stage Plays) Limited, which controlled the theatre. When the theatre changed hands in 1971 he was able to sell these shares for a capital sum which produced an income equivalent to a pension. He died in 1977. His widow, Winifred Keates, has a large collection of material relating to the Theatre Royal which was collected by Jack Keates throughout his life.

A new Managing Director naturally had to be found. Glynne Burnand, who was a Director of both theatre companies, persuaded the Directors to offer the position to Melville Gillam of the Connaught Theatre, Worthing. The latter accepted the offer and took up his duties on 12th February 1963. The first play shown under his management, though no doubt booked long beforehand by Baxter Somerville, was *Mary, Mary* by Jean Kerr.

Like most theatre managers, Melville Gillam started life on the stage and was trained at the Birmingham Repertory Company. He then took the lease of a theatre of his own at Lye in Worcestershire, where he presented variety shows, pantomimes and repertory plays. After the intervention of the war he moved to Worthing. The Connaught Theatre there had been used by the Rank

Organisation for training film actors. A group of local business men bought the theatre, and Melville Gillam became its Managing Director, producer and director of plays. He established there a repertory company which became as well-known for the training of future stars as had been the Theatre Royal, Brighton, before it. Amongst others, Susannah York, Daniel Massey, Peter Bryne, Sarah Miles and Glenda Jackson started their careers there. Guest directors such as Peter Hall and John Schlesinger also produced plays for him there.

The new Managing Director continued Baxter Somerville's policy of showing the best London and travelling productions that were available, and the year 1963 proved little different in quality from the preceding years. On 1st July John Gielgud, Irene Worth and Marie Löhr played in *The Ides of March* by Jerome Kilty. On 19th August Charles Boyer made one of his rare appearances on the English stage in a new play by Terence Rattigan, *Man and Boy*. At about that time Rattigan became a Brighton resident and lived for a few years at No. 79 Marine Parade. Sybil Thorndike and Lewis Casson visited the theatre during the week of 7th October in *Queen Bee* by Judith Guthrie. Flora Robson, Donald Wolfit and Margaret Rawlings appeared in *John Gabriel Borkman* during the week of 25th November. The year ended with the most un-Christmaslike play imaginable: *The Father* by Strindberg, with Trevor Howard and Joyce Redman.

In 1964 Sybil Thorndike made two more appearances: on 5th January in one of William Douglas Home's comedies, *The Reluctant Peer*, which was about his brother, Sir Alec or Lord Home; and on 10th August with Gwen Ffrangcon-Davies and Paul Rogers in *Season of Goodwill* by Arthur Marshall. Probably the outstanding event of the year consisted of the two Shakespeare plays sponsored by the British Council which were shown in Brighton prior to the tour in South America. These were *The Merchant of Venice* and *A Midsummer Night's Dream,* with Ralph Richardson and Barbara Jefford. Richardson gave a notable performance as Shylock. He made a second appearance at the theatre that year on 31st August in *Carving a Statue* by Graham Greene. In a play called *Maxibules,* which was translated from the French of Marcel Aymé by Kitty Black and shown on 23rd November, Max

Adrian gave a remarkable exhibition of versatility by playing about thirteen different parts, including several women.

During this year (1964) the municipal authorities again insisted on the re-arrangement of seats in the auditorium in order to satisfy the fire precautions, and the centre gangway was removed from the front section of the stalls.

The early part of 1965 brought two plays of the new vogue: *Inadmissible Evidence* by John Osborne, with Nichol Williamson on 8th March and the Royal Shakespeare Company's production of *The Homecoming* by Harold Pinter on 26th April. The latter was followed by Enid Bagnold's third play *The Chinese Prime Minister*, with Edith Evans and Brian Aherne. The week of 2nd August saw another one-woman show in the person of Marlene Dietrich. Chekhov's less well-known play *Ivanov* was given on 6th September with John Gielgud, Claire Bloom and Yvonne Mitchell. The year ended with two plays by Shaw: *Getting Married* on 13th December and *You Never Can Tell* on 23rd December with Ralph Richardson and Judy Campbell.

1966 began with a new play by Arthur Miller, *Incident at Vichy* with Alec Guiness and Anthony Quayle. A revival of *Arsenic and Old Lace* by Joseph Kesselring brought Sybil Thorndike and Athene Seyler back to the theatre on 14th February. But the principal feature of the year was perhaps three one-man or woman shows. On 14th March Peggy Ashcroft gave a recital in prose and verse called *Portraits of Women*. On 4th April Michael Mac Liammoir returned with *The Importance of Being Oscar*, alternated with a programme comprising a history of Ireland as seen through the eyes of her poets, wits, sons and daughters, which he called *I Must Be Talking to My Friends*. On 21st November Marlene Dietrich made a second visit. Other notable events of the year were Vanessa Redgrave in *The Prime of Miss Jean Brodie* by J. Presson Allen on 11th April; Glynis Johns and Keith Mitchell, making his first appearance as Henry VIII, in *The King's Mare* on 20th June; Coral Browne, Isobel Jeans, Juliet Mills and Wilfred Hyde White in *Lady Windermere's Fan* on 23rd August; Ralph Richardson and Margaret Rutherford in *The Rivals* on 20th September; and in complete contrast Paul Scofield and Patrick Magee in the world premiere of *The Staircase* by Charles Dyer on 25th October.

During 1966 Lord Cohen of Brighton, who had been Chairman of both theatre companies since 1961, died. He was succeeded as Chairman by A. E. Brocke, who held the office until his own death in September 1969. A. E. Russell then took his place for the following year. Two months before Lord Cohen died R. C. Pascoe, the senior partner of Howlett and Clarke, of No. 8 Ship Street, Brighton, the oldest firm of solicitors in the town, joined the Board of Theatre Royal Brighton (Stage Plays) Ltd., but not apparently of the Brighton Theatre Royal Company. Similarly Lord Cohen's place as a Director was taken in June 1967 by his widow, Lady Cohen of Brighton. Lady Cohen was the daughter of Simon Frieze and the widow of Leonard Bodlander. She had married Lord Cohen as his second wife in 1961.

The highlight of 1967 was the first visit to Brighton of the National Theatre Company during the week of 17th April. This was the year of the first Brighton Festival of Music, and the National Company's visit was the Theatre Royal's contribution to the first week of this Festival. The Company presented two plays: Strindberg's *The Dance of Death* and one of Georges Feydeau's deplorable farces that are now so popular, *A Flea in Her Ear*. In the former Laurence Olivier made one of his rare appearances at the Theatre Royal, though he was by then an established resident of Royal Crescent. Geraldine McEwan played opposite him. In the second week of the Brighton Festival the theatre presented a new play by Robert Bolt called *Brother and Sister* with Flora Robson, Laurence Naismith and Nigel Stock. About five years before this Flora Robson, who had lived in Hove as a girl, had again become a Brighton resident and had taken a house in Marine Gardens, Kemp Town.

Two months after the Brighton Festival the Royal Shakespeare Company made a visit of two weeks. They presented two plays: *Ghosts*, in which Peggy Ashcroft played the principal part and *Little Murders* with Barbara Jefford and Brenda Bruce.

1968 was a year of great variety, both in old and new plays and in the performance of senior and junior actors. The year began and ended with an old play. On 23rd January Flora Robson made another visit, this time with *The Importance of Being Earnest*, assisted by Robert Eddison, Isobel Jeans, John Standing and

Daniel Massey. At the end of the year, 9th December Tommy Steele played in Carlo Goldoni's old comedy *A Servant of Two Masters*. On 19th February Sybil Thorndike made her last appearance in the Theatre Royal in another play by Enid Bagnold, *Call Me Jacky*. A new star appeared at the theatre for the first time during the year. This was Ian McKellen, who actually made two visits: on 5th February in two short plays by Peter Shaffer, *The White Liars* and *Black Comedy* and on 11th November in *Arms and the Man* and *Richard II*. New dramatists were represented by John Osborne, who had two plays produced, *Time Present* on 13th May and *The Hotel in Amsterdam* on 24th June and by Alan Bennett in *Forty Years On* on 14th October. Jill Bennett starred in the first of these, Paul Scofield in the second and John Gielgud in the third. The year was completed by another visit from the National Theatre Company but this time without Laurence Olivier. Joan Plowright appeared in *The Advertisement* by Natalia Ginsburg, translated by Henry Reed, and Robert Stephens and Geraldine McEwan in *Home and Beauty* by Somerset Maugham.

The first event of importance in 1969 was the visit of the Royal Shakespeare Company on 17th March in the world première of *Dutch Uncle* by Simon Gray. Maggie Fitzgibbon took the title role in *Candida* on 30th June. A third and more notable visit by the National Theatre Company took place during the week of 29th September. They played *The Three Sisters* and *The Way of the World*. Laurence Olivier appeared in the former but only in the relatively small part of Dr. Chibutikin. On 24th November a new play by Robin Maugham (Viscount Maugham) called *Enemy* was produced. Robin Maugham at that time was a Brighton resident, living at No. 25 Lewes Crescent. The year ended with the production of *Oh! What a Lovely War!* by Theatre Workshop and Charles Chilton with the original London cast. The film of this play was afterwards to be made in Brighton, largely on the West Pier.

On 20th January 1970 John Gielgud, Patrick Magee and Wendy Hiller struggled with a difficult play by Peter Shaffer called *The Battle of Shrivings*. On 21st April Raymond Massey made one of his rare post-war appearances in England and came to Brighton with a play by Robert Anderson called *I Never Sang To My Father*. The theatre's contributions to the Brighton Festival that year, from 6th to 17th May were: *Abelard and Heloise* by Ronald Miller, with Diana Rigg and Keith Michell, and *It's Underneath That Counts* by John Wilding. On 8th June John Gielgud made another visit this time with Ralph Richardson, in *Home* by David Storey. A more cheerful new play on 20th July was *How the Other Half Loves* by Alan Ayckbourn with Robert Morley. The Cambridge Theatre Company, which included Ian McKellen, brought two plays to the theatre during the week of 2nd November: Farquhar's *The Recruiting Officer* and *Chips With Everything* by Arnold Wesker. The year ended with a reversion to the old policy of staging a pantomime or traditional Christmas play. In this production, *Goldilocks and the Three Bears*, another Brighton resident of long standing, Dora Bryan, played the principal part.

1st February 1971 saw another rare visitor to England, Ingrid Bergman in *Captain Brassbound's Conversion*. On 29th March the Oxford Playhouse Company brought *The Merry Wives of Windsor*. During the first week in May, as part of the current Brighton Festival, the Phoenix Opera Company produced *The Barber of Seville* with Ian Wallace and Soo-Bee-Lee and *Albert Herring* with Sylvia Fisher. The following week Ian McKellen appeared in *Hamlet*. On the 24th May the D'Oyly Carte Opera Company made a re-appearance at the theatre for the first time since 1934. During their visit of two weeks they even revived *The Sorcerer* which is the least played of all the usual Gilbert and Sullivan operas. On 26th July Alec Guiness and Jeremy Brett appeared in *Journey Round My Father* by John Mortimer. On 19th October John Clements brought the Chichester Festival production of *Dear Antoine* by Jean Anouilh. The Christmas play was again a traditional one: *A Christmas Carol* with Richard Todd.

On 16th December 1971 the theatre changed hands. Since 1962 all the shares in the landlord company, Brighton Theatre Royal Limited, had been in the hands of the tenant company, Theatre Royal Brighton (Stage Plays) Limited. Of the shares in the latter company, 20 had been allotted to Jack Keates in lieu of a pension. The remaining 200 were owned in equal shares by four directors, Lord Cohen, Glynne Burnand, A. E. Brocke and A. E. Russell. Lord Cohen and A. E. Brooke had since died and so were represented by their executors. All these five shareholders were now bought out by another theatre company named Louis I. Michaels Limited at the price of £1,000 a share or £230,000 in all. This company was run by a theatre proprietor named Louis Michaels. He had originally been the owner of a chain of boutiques named Chanelle and had later owned large stores in Bournemouth, Bath and Cheltenham, which he had subsequently sold. The first theatre which he purchased was the Playhouse at Bournemouth. He then went on to present plays with Harold Fielding. The Theatre Royal at Brighton was the second theatre which he acquired. Since 1971 he has come to own the Richmond Theatre at Richmond, Surrey; the Theatre Royal at Bath; the Devonshire Park Theatre at Eastbourne and the Haymarket Theatre in London. He has formed another company for the productions of plays named Triumph Theatre Productions Limited which operates from the Ivor Novello Suite at the Strand Theatre. This company has subsequently presented plays all over England and, outside Great Britain as far afield as the United States, Canada, South Africa, Hong Kong and Australia.

Two changes were made in the Board of Directors of both theatre companies when the theatre changed hands. A. E. Russell and Glynne Burnand resigned. Louis Michaels took A. E. Russell's place as Chairman of both companies. Melville Gillam remained Managing Director. Therefore there was no change in the policy of the theatre. The other two Directors, Lady Cohen of Brighton and R. C. Pascoe, also remained in office.

The first important play to be shown in 1972 was another Chichester Festival production, Margaret Leighton and Nigel Patrick in *Reunion in Vienna* by Robert Sherwood. Three weeks later John Gielgud and John Mills played together in *Veterans* by Charles Wood. As the theatre's contribution to the Brighton Festival of that year the Royal Swedish Opera from the Court Theatre at Drottningholm, Stockholm, and the Royal Swedish Ballet made a visit of two weeks from 11th May. Elizabeth Söderstrom and Kerstin Meyer sang in *Cosi Fan Tutte* and in Gluck's *Orfeo*. The following week saw the unusual revival of what is now probably J. M. Barrie's least produced play, *Mary Rose*, with Mia Farrow. The week of 3rd July was given to the English Royal Ballet. On 11th September there was a visit from a film star not often seen on the English stage, Deborah Kerr. She played in *The Day After the Fair* adapted by Frank Harvey from a short story by Thomas Hardy named *On the Western Circuit.* A fortnight later Eileen Atkins appeared in a difficult play named *Suzanne Andler,* translated by Barbara Bray from thc French of Marguerite Duras. The most notable productions of the last quarter of the year were two one-man or woman shows: Joyce Grenfell in *Monologues and Songs, Old and New* 30th October and the great French mime, Marcel Marceau, on 13th November.

The re-appearance of *Mary Rose* was perhaps the beginning of a modest Barrie revival, as on 27th February 1973 another of his plays which was less out of fashion, *What Every Woman Knows,* followed with Dorothy Tutin and Cathleen Nesbitt. 12th March saw another one-man show in Roy Dotrice playing in *Aubrey's Brief Lives.* The fortnight of the Brighton Festival from 9th May was entirely given to ballet, the New London Ballet and the Royal Ballet with Margot Fonteyn as a guest artist. Two weeks later Marlene Dietrich made a third visit to Brighton. The next week the Royal Shakespeare Company presented Peggy Ashcroft in two plays by Harold Pinter: *Landscape* and *A Slight Ache.* During the rest of the year most of the productions of note were revivals of classics, such as *Arms and the Man* with Jenny Agutter and Tom Courtenay on 25th June and *The Constant Wife* by Somerset Maugham with Ingrid Bergman on 27th August. The Actors Company with Ian McKellen brought two plays on 24th September: *The Way of the World* and Chekhov's less well known *The Wood Demon.* A fortnight later Edith Evans made her last appearance at the Theatre Royal in a recital of her favourite roles and pieces: *Edith Evans and Friends.*

In August of that year (1973) the Theatre Royal suffered the loss of a devoted servant who was a familiar figure not only to theatregoers but to some of the public beyond the walls of the theatre. This was Bill Tupper, who had been on the staff of the theatre since 1920 in Lawson Lambert's days. During that period he had carried out all sorts of jobs, but he was best known, at least in the last twenty years of his life, as the commissionaire who called out the numbers for patrons' cars at the end of the performances. His magnificent voice could easily be heard in the Royal Pavilion across the intervening gardens. His best vocal performance was the medical 'ninety-nine', and it was remarkable how many of the people who made use of his services seemed to live in a house or have a taxi of that number! Since his time car numbers have not been called out, and New Road is the poorer for the disappearance of a colourful local character of long standing.

1974 was perhaps not so prolific in outstanding productions as other years at this period. The Brighton Festival began on 8th May. The theatre's contribution was a visit from the Phoenix Opera Company in Offenbach's *La Vie Parisienne* during the first week and the National Theatre Company in *Next of Kin* by John Hopkins during the second week. The National Theatre actually made a second visit to Brighton in 1974 in the week of 24th June, when Joan Plowright played in *Eden End* by J. B. Priestley. This was the beginning of a modest revival of Priestley's work, as 1972-3 had been for Barrie, and on 2nd December Barbara Jefford and Rachel Gurney played in *Dangerous Corner.*

The beginning of 1975 saw two one-man shows: Emlyn Williams making a return visit in his readings from Charles Dickens on 27th January, and *A Funny Kind of Evening* with David Kossoff on 3rd February. Alec Guinness and Margaret Leighton appeared on 17th March in *A Family and a Fortune,* dramatised by Julian Michell from the novel of Ivy Compton Burnett, who had lived in Hove as a young woman. The Brighton Festival on 6th May comprised both drama and opera: the Festival Actors Company in Moliere's *Tartuffe* during the first week and the Welsh National Opera Company during the second week with Puccini's *Manon Lescaut* and Offenbach's *La Grande Duchesse de Geroldstein.* On 1st September Anna Neagle appeared in a play by William Douglas Home, *The Dame of Sark,* and on 20th of that month the Royal Ballet Company made another visit.

Early in the following year (1976) Margot Fonteyn made two special appearances on 22nd and 23rd January with the New London Ballet Company. Ten days later John Mills and Moira Lister played in a musical version of *Great Expectations.* The theatre's contribution to the Brighton Festival that year was entirely operatic. During the week of 4th May the English Music Theatre Company presented a comedy for music in three acts named *Tom Jones* by Stephen Oliver, Rossini's *Cinderella* and *The Turn of the Screw* by Benjamin Britten, in which the chief singer was Anthony Rolfe Johnson. In the second week the Ludwigsburg Festival Opera presented *The Magic Flute,* and Michael Aspinall made one appearance as *The Surprising Soprano.* In the week following the festival John Clements and Anna Neagle appeared in a revival of *The First Mrs Fraser,* which St John Ervine had written for Marie Tempest and Henry Ainley before the war of 1939. The week of 7th June saw a production of *The Three Sisters* with Janet Suzman, Angela Down, Susan Engel, Nigel Davenport and Sebastian Shaw. On 19th July Max Bygraves gave a one-man show for a whole week. This was followed by a four week's season of the television serial *Dad's Army,* with Arthur Lowe and John Le Mesurier. After this Douglas Fairbanks Junior made his only appearance in Brighton with *The Pleasure of His Company* by Samuel Taylor. The last show of note during that year was *An Ideal Husband* on 6th December with Wilfred Hyde White, Sylvia Simms, Edward Hardwicke and Rachel Gurney.

Early in 1977 (21st February) Glenda Jackson appeared in a play about the poetess Stevie Smith called *Stevie.* A month later there was an event which by then had become rare in Brighton, namely a Shakespeare production. Joss Ackland and Wendy Craig acted in *The Taming of the Shrew.* On 18th April for two weeks William Douglas Home's latest play *The Kingfisher* was played by Ralph Richardson, Celia Johnson and Alan Webb. After this Janet Suzman appeared in *Hedda Gabler.* For the first three weeks of June the D'Oyly Carte Opera Company made their annual visit, but with only five operas. The occasion was, however, remarkable for an unusual circumstance. There was no performance at the Theatre Royal on 16th June because on that day the company was transported by motor coach to Windsor Castle, where they gave a command performance of *H.M.S. Pinafore* in the Waterloo Chamber, before the Queen and her guests. A precedent for this had occurred as far back as 6th March 1891, when the D'Oyly Carte Company had given a command performance of *The Gondoliers* before Queen Victoria, also in the Waterloo Chamber at Windsor Castle. It was an appropriate coincidence that, during the Company's visit to Brighton in 1977, their principal singer

John Reed, who played George Grossmith's and Henry Lytton's roles in all the operas, was awarded the OBE in the Queen's Birthday Honours of the Jubilee year.

The Brighton Festival in 1977 was unaccountably and most unsuitably moved from May to July. During its first week (4th July) the theatre was occupied by the Frankfurt Ballet from Germany. During the second week (12th July) Susan Hampshire and Richard Pasco appeared in *Man and Superman*. The week of 12th September saw a revival of Somerset Maugham's *The Sacred Flame*, in which the part played by Gladys Cooper in the revival of June 1966, was taken by Jean Anderson, another Brighton resident of some years' standing. With her in this play was another actor who had Brighton connections, Macdonald Hobley. His father had been Vicar of St. Andrew's Old Parish Church, Hove. He was educated at Brighton College and while there succeeded to the principal position in its dramatic corps that had been left vacant by his immediate predecessors, Christopher Hassell and Michael Hordern. On leaving school he became a BBC announcer and proceeded via that profession to the stage.

On 3rd October Robert Morley gave a week's solo performance which he called *Robert Morley talks to Everyone*. Towards the end of the year (27th November) another Shakespeare play, *Romeo and Juliet*, was played. This established somewhat of a record for recent years of two separate Shakespearean productions during a single year. One hopes that it is a precedent for future years.

EPILOGUE

HAVING arrived at the present day it is reasonable to ask: 'What of the future?' The Theatre Royal today is in good shape, seems prosperous, presents the best shows available in the provincial theatre, despite the fact that the present is not an inspiring period for the quality of new plays, and still fulfils a vital part in Brighton life. But, like all cultural activities, it is always dependent on the ever increasing demands of the Chancellor of the Exchequer and the fickle taste of the public. In earlier periods it was entertainment tax which crippled theatrical managements. Today value added tax stands in its place, and cultural entertainment secures no zero rating from this. Like other provincial theatres, no financial help is received from the Arts Council of Great Britain.

At the moment the public seems fairly faithful to the theatres in general. Twenty-five years ago, at the time when the St James's Theatre in London was demolished, it was said that no new theatres would ever be built in England. However, several have not only been built but are reasonably prosperous. Others, however, have gone out of existence as theatres. Some of these have only been converted into bingo-halls, from which they could again be rescued in the future, as in the past other theatres have been saved from similar ignoble uses. But some have actually been demolished to make way for more profitable property development. This a permanent loss. But if at the height of the cinema boom anyone had prophesied that the theatre would outlive the cinema and see the latter shrink to very small proportions he would probably not have been believed. We have lived to see this happen. Television has largely taken the place of the cinema. But the theatre retains its pre-cinema distinction. It is up to the public to see that this remains so. In Brighton the Theatre Royal has enriched cultural life for many generations. One can hardly think of the town without it. We can only hope that, as it has survived the various trials of the last one hundred and seventy years which are related in this book, it will continue to go from strength to strength during the next one hundred and seventy years.